American Academy of
Orthopaedic Surgeons

AAOS American Association of
Orthopaedic Surgeons

Managing Orthopaedic Malpractice Risk

2nd edition

Prepared by
the Committee on Professional Liability

Managing Orthopaedic Malpractice Risk,
second edition
American Academy of Orthopaedic Surgeons

The material presented in *Managing Orthopaedic Malpractice* Risk, Second Edition, has been made available by the American Academy of Orthopaedic Surgeons for educational purposes only. This material is not intended to present the only, or necessarily best, methods or procedures for the medical situations discussed, but rather is intended to represent an approach, view, statement, or opinion of the author(s) or producer(s), which may be helpful to others who face similar situations.

Second Edition
Copyright © 2000 by the
American Academy of Orthopaedic Surgeons

ISBN: 0-89203-249-9

American Academy of Orthopaedic Surgeons Staff

Kristin Olds Glavin, JD
Associate General Counsel

Marilyn Fox, PhD
Director of Publications

Paul Psilos, PhD
Manufacturing Manager

Loraine Edwalds, MBA
Production Manager

Lexine Cramm
Legal Secretary

Table of Contents

Preface

This 2nd Edition text was prepared by the American Academy of Orthopaedic Surgeons Committee on Professional Liability with two goals intended: to help orthopaedic surgeons provide the highest possible quality care and clinical outcomes to patients; and to reduce the risk of successful lawsuits. Toward these ends the Committee has reviewed the database of PIAA (Physician Insurers Association of America) to identify diagnoses and/or procedures which produce frequent and expensive losses for orthopaedic surgeons; and has conducted studies of closed claims at various physician-owned malpractice insurers across the country over the past ten years to determine specific issues associated with these losses. The studies cited represent an expansion and continuation of the Committee's prior efforts.

The principles presented are not intended to serve as standard of care guidelines, nor as absolute models of appropriate conduct. We have noted some general principles which are intended to reduce risk, and have addressed the salient issues associated with each procedure or diagnosis that has emerged from our closed claim studies. The principles cited and discussed are intended as informational and educational tools to enhance quality patient care and safety. The orthopaedist's professional judgment remains foremost in the delivery of quality care. We believe this text will assist in the processes of quality care as well as minimize malpractice risk.

The American Academy of Orthopaedic Surgeons is deeply indebted to Lori Bartholomew, Loss Prevention and Research Consultant of Physician Insurers Association of American (PIAA), and to Kristin Olds Glavin, JD, AAOS Associate General Counsel and staff liaison to the Committee on Professional Liability.

Special appreciation is extended to those PIAA member companies which facilitated committee studies on-site at their offices, and those that cooperated in the AAOS-PIAA data collection process.

We hope that you find this text useful professionally, and we hope it is beneficial to your patients.

Committee on Professional Liability

Steven S. Fountain, MD, Chair

Dennis B. Brooks, MD

Dale R. Butler, MD

Jack C. Childers, Jr., MD

Allen S. Edmonson, MD

Morton Farber, MD

Lynn C. Garner, MD

K. Mason Howard, MD

Maureen K. Molloy, MD

Albert E. Sanders, MD

Charles A. Webb, MD

Anthony T. Yeung, MD

Kristin Olds Glavin, JD, Staff Liaison

PIAA Member Companies Participating in Claims Study and Data Collection

Mutual Insurance Company of Arizona

Medical Insurance Exchange of California

NORCAL Mutual Insurance Company — California

COPIC Insurance Company — Colorado

Physicians Protective Trust Company — Florida

MAG Mutual Insurance Company — Georgia

Illinois State Medical Inter-Insurance Exchange

Kansas Medical Mutual Company

Kentucky Medical Insurance Company

Louisiana Medical Mutual Insurance Company

Medical Mutual Insurance Company of Maine

Medical Mutual Liability Insurance Society of Maryland

Medical Professional Mutual Insurance Company — Massachusetts

Midwest Medical Insurance Company — Minnesota

Missouri Medical Insurance Company

Medical Defense Associates — Missouri

New Mexico Physicians Mutual Liability

Medical Liability Mutual — New York

Medical Mutual Insurance Company of North Carolina

Physicians Insurance Company of Ohio

Physicians Liability Insurance Company of Oklahoma

Pennsylvania Medical Society Liability Insurance Company

State Volunteer Mutual Insurance Company — Tennessee

Utah Medical Insurance Association

National Capital Reciprocal Insurance Company — Washington, DC

Physicians Insurance Exchange — Washington

Introduction

The Orthopaedic Surgeon's principal goal is the provision of optimum quality patient care

Occasionally a patient perceives the care rendered to be below the expected standard; the claim may or may not be meritorious. Most orthopaedists will face a malpractice claim during their career. The AAOS Committee on Professional Liability has developed this second edition of *Managing Orthopaedic Malpractice Risk* to assist the orthopaedic surgeon identify factors which may cause a patient to file a lawsuit, including patient dissatisfaction, as well as to identify procedures and diagnoses that have historically been the most common to produce legal action or which have proven most expensive to resolve.

The chapter on general issues addresses many elements common to all malpractice lawsuits, including factors which lead the patient to sue; informed consent; system issues associated with the suits; and specific commentary on issues directly affecting the defensibility of claims.

The committee has conducted studies of closed claims for several diagnoses, surgical procedures and age groups. Each study was designed to elicit general information and conclusions from the data, and to determine specific findings or actions or omissions which were critical to the filing of a lawsuit and perhaps to its eventual outcome. Specific areas of focus include:

- ◆ **Common Threads and Practical Applications**
- ◆ **Failure to Diagnose**
- ◆ **Femoral Neck & Intertrochanteric Fractures**
- ◆ **Femur Fractures**
- ◆ **Foot and Ankle**
- ◆ **Knee Arthroscopy**
- ◆ **Pediatric Orthopaedics**
- ◆ **Shoulder**
- ◆ **Spine Surgery**
- ◆ **Tibia Fractures**
- ◆ **Total Joint**

The following allegations associated with these lawsuits are listed in order of decreasing frequency:

- ◆ poor surgical performance
- ◆ failure to diagnose the patient's condition
- ◆ postoperative infection
- ◆ failure to diagnose or properly manage complications
- ◆ technical complications.

Based on 2,640 claims against orthopaedists resolved by the PIAA in the years 1996-1998:

Defending an orthopaedic claim related to spine surgery was most costly, with average defense costs of $47,291, compared with all other claims which generated defense costs averaging $19,648.

Indemnity payments to patients (and their lawyers) were highest for spine surgery other than fusion, averaging $295,842. The lowest indemnity payments were awarded for claims resulting from arthroscopy, which averaged $135,764.

With both indemnity payments and defense costs considered, several findings are evident. Claims arising from spine surgery (other than fusion) and spinal fusion generated both the highest indemnity payments and the two highest categories of defense costs; thus, either form of spine surgery appears to be associated with significant potential risk. Claims resulting from knee arthroscopy showed the lowest indemnity payments and defense costs.

General Results

Analysis of claims revealed that most were resolved without trial, and most were resolved without payment to the plaintiff. PIAA data from 1996-1998 showed that:

58%	were settled without indemnity payment
25%	were settled with indemnity payment
8%	were dismissed by the court
6%	went to trial with defense verdict
2%	went to trial with plaintiff verdict
0.7%	were arbitrated or mediated with indemnity payment
0.3%	were arbitrated or mediated without indemnity payment

Common Threads and Practical Applications

The Committee on Professional Liability has conducted detailed reviews of hundreds of malpractice claims, successful and unsuccessful, relating to almost every major facet of orthopaedic surgery. In a sense, there is some lesson to be learned from every claim. However, for the most part these lessons fall into two broad groups: general principles, often well known to orthopaedists but which continue to cause claims; and specific causes applicable to certain diagnoses, operations, or clinical situations. They will be discussed under those headings.

Generally applicable lessons we have (repeatedly) learned

1. Informed Consent. We continue to find claims based on lack of informed consent. We recognize that it is not possible for many patients to fully grasp all the implications of every possible eventuality, and even if it were possible, the patient will not remember a substantial portion of it several months later. Furthermore, it is often not practical for the surgeon to document every word said during the discussion. Fortunately, this is not necessary. Typically, in order to sustain a claim on the basis of lack of informed consent, the plaintiff must establish three things:

   a. Some item of information was not given,

   b. If the plaintiff had been given that information, he/she (or the hypothetical "reasonable patient") would not have consented, and

   c. Harm resulted from giving the consent.

   The first of these is difficult to defend, usually degenerating into a contest as to who the jury believes said or didn't say what. However, if the surgeon thoroughly explains (and documents) at least one horrible possible outcome (including the possibility of death), the defense attorney has a powerful tool to attack the second. ("Do you mean to tell me, Mr. Plaintiff, that you were willing to risk death, but if you had known about complication X you wouldn't have been willing to risk that?")

2. Wrong site surgery. We continue to find claims for operating on the wrong site. We estimate this occurred once in every 7,400 knee arthroscopies in 1992 despite what seem to many to be adequate safeguards. (There were an estimated 1,200,000[!] arthroscopies that year.) We believe the AAOS "Sign your Site" initiative will reduce this number and strongly urge every orthopaedist to read the Academy's statement and comply with it. The crucial factor is for the surgeon to see and speak with the patient on the day of surgery, and for the surgeon to mark the site *while the patient is fully alert.*

3. Failure/Delay in diagnosis or treatment. There are two major types:

   a. Trauma. The most frequent sites were cervical spine, femoral neck, and syndesmotic injuries of the ankle. Be especially wary when an injury in any of these areas looks worse clinically than can be accounted for on images.

   b. Claims for damages due to postoperative complications such as infection or pulmonary embolus. These are usually easily defended as recognized risks of the procedure *unless there was delay in diagnosing and treating* the complications. Be on guard against the natural human tendency to deny disagreeable events, and vigorously pursue diagnosis and treatment as soon as there is any suspicion. Alternatively, include in the post-op orders automatic triggers such as "CBC if Tmax exceeds 38.5 on two successive days." The important consideration is not what the specific parameters of the trigger are, but that they are there.

   An emerging source of claims is failure to diagnose Lyme disease. Remember that it can co-exist with other joint afflictions.

4. Complications under casts still occur. We can only repeat the old maxim: "There are no hypochondriacs under casts." *All complaints under casts should be taken seriously and investigated aggressively and immediately.* This is especially true in cases of tibial fractures where compartment syndromes make nonsurgical treatment, on average, more costly in terms of malpractice indemnity per case than surgical treatment.

5. It should be unnecessary to mention, but we still encounter cases of medical record alteration. Moral considerations aside, there are two factors which should be pondered by any surgeon so tempted:

   a. There are so many organizations (legally) perusing and copying pages of charts that there is a high probability that somewhere there will be a copy of any page containing an antedated note made *before the antedated note was inserted.*

   b. Modern techniques of determining just when pen met paper are sophisticated beyond the imagination of most non-law enforcement personnel. We have seen cases that otherwise would have been perfectly defensible settled for large sums because of apparently altered records, even when the guilty party was not known.

Lessons applicable to specific circumstances

1. Make *sure* that pre-op THR patients know that their leg lengths may not be equal.

2. When post-op THR patients have sciatic neuropraxia, the defense attorney should delay for at least a year, then ask for an independent medical examination. Most neuropraxias are due to stretch and will abate within a year.

3. Blade-plate and screw-plate devices are generally not intended for use in subtrochanteric fractures and many are packaged with specific disclaimers. This leaves a surgeon all but defenseless if their use results in failure and/or nonunion.

4. External rotation deformities following femur fractures in older children often resulted in very large jury verdicts even when there seemed to be little or no functional impairment.

5. Early conversion of failed internal fixation of femoral neck fractures to femoral

head replacement resulted in a high incidence of post-op infection. Wait at least two weeks, if at all possible.

6. Closed tibial fractures treated with casts always heal with the same amount of shortening and rotation they had when first seen. If such treatment is elected, the patient and family should be prepared for this outcome, and the discussion should be documented and, preferably, witnessed.

7. Spinal surgery patients often did not seem adequately apprised that their pain might not be relieved by the procedure. Failure to improve was a frequent cause of claim. In the claims that were successful, there was a pattern of lack of objective physical findings at the preoperative examination and a lack of correlation between physical findings with the level and extent of disease found in imaging studies.

8. Wrong level spine surgery still occurs frequently enough to show that existing procedures to identify the level are not failsafe.

9. As late as the mid 1980's, we were still encountering claims made for bimalleolar fractures in which internal fixation of only one side was performed and the fixation failed.

10. Pilon and syndesmotic injuries of the ankle are prone to poor results. Only experienced trauma surgeons should attempt open treatment, and the patient, especially young active patients, should be prepared for a less than fully functional result.

11. Failure to reduce dislocations or significant subluxations of ankle fractures while awaiting open treatment may produce skin sloughs or actual opening of the fracture. The need to avoid this risk would seem obvious, but we still encounter cases.

12. The most common cause of claim in bunion surgery was postoperative misalignment, in multiple hammertoes it was wrong site, and in foot injuries it was missed Lisfranc dislocation/fractures. Be especially wary in these situations.

In summary, although we have found, and continue to find, unusual or even counter intuitive causes of malpractice claims, most continue to be based on errors or misjudgments of principles well known to the orthopaedic community. It is our hope that by raising the level of awareness among orthopaedists of these principles the number of claims will be reduced along with the resulting cost, anxiety, and legal adversity.

Review of Specific Diagnoses and Procedures

Failure to Diagnose

Introduction

Allegations of failure to timely diagnose various conditions occurred as a common thread in many different studies of malpractice claims, leading to a study of this topic specifically. This involved review of hundreds of malpractice claims from several insurance carriers. The reviewers felt that there was true malpractice in 32%, and no malpractice in 58%, and they were unable to reach a determination in 10% of the cases. The following suggestions are loosely grouped by condition, type of patient, and clinical setting.

Trauma-Fracture

1. Review or obtain radiographs at time of first visit.

2. Be quick to order additional images.

3. Read "the edges" of all images.

4. Don't take the word of others that the images are negative.

5. Revisit patients with polytrauma. Suspect additional injuries not at first apparent. Beware of nonskeletal injuries.

6. Examine the entire extremity or extremities involved.

7. Visualize C7- T1 on all cervical injury patients.

8. Be suspicious of foreign body if drainage persists after open fracture.

9. Remove cast if necessary to adequately examine patient with symptoms of deep venous thrombosis (DVT).

10. Suspect scapholunate instability, Lisfranc dislocations, and lesser toe dislocations if swelling is out of proportion to soft-tissue injury.

11. If antibiotics are started in suspected infections, do not stop until culture results are back.

Difficult-to-Evaluate Patients

Certain categories of patients require more meticulous evaluation:

1. Pediatric patients. Most common missed diagnoses are avascular necrosis, congenital dislocation of the hip, slipped capital femoral epiphysis, and neoplasm. If any of these are suspected but not verified by imaging, protect the patient, warn the family, and reevaluate at appropriate intervals.

2. Elderly patients. Most commonly missed diagnoses are fracture and neoplasm. Insist on good images, including MRIs or bone scans if pathology is not apparent on plain films. Be quick to get a second opinion.

3. Obtunded or psychiatrically impaired patients. Obscure diagnoses in these patients can be especially challenging. Keep in mind that absence of history of illness may be misleading. A physician

who fails to at least attempt to follow up patients who miss appointments may be held liable.

Perioperative

1. Patients at increased risk, such as diabetics, should have their preoperative status carefully evaluated and documented. Pre-op consent should include and document thorough explanation of increased risk.

2. Postoperative complications, even apparently minor ones, should be aggressively diagnosed and treated. Resist the tendency to ignore potentially disagreeable events.

3. If you suspect a postoperative complication, inform the patient and family early rather than late of your suspicion and what you are doing to diagnose or treat it. Patients who suspect you are minimizing or, worse, concealing such information are likely to be very unforgiving if the outcome is serious.

4. Review all x-rays and laboratory tests you order.

Other

1. **Don't** alter records, or make any notations that could be construed as alterations. This should be unnecessary to say, but our reviews of recent closed claims still demonstrate these cases.

2. Compartment syndrome, or impending compartment syndrome, is a true emergency.

3. There is no substitute for a well worded, clear, informed consent.

4. Obtain a second opinion early if the patient is not doing well. Obtain consultation sooner rather than later when you can't explain a patient's complaint or symptoms.

5. Identify patients at risk for DVT, and consider prophylaxis.

6. Do your own pre- and post-op care, if possible. No one else will have the same rapport or empathy.

Femur Fractures Other Than Intertrochanteric

Complications

Closed treatment of children's fractures resulted in the most frequent and expensive complications, including foot drop, skin loss, compartment syndrome, and malrotation/shortening. In adults, common complications included poor technique (inappropriate fixation, early hardware removal, malrotation), infection (especially a problem when not recognized early and/or proper consultation not obtained), wrong site surgery, fat and/or pulmonary embolism, and delay in diagnosis or treatment.

Additional complications resulted from the use of plates and screws for subtrochanteric fractures despite package insert warnings to the contrary, undersized intramedullary rods, and poor hardware selection (plates/screws) in other regions of the femur.

Introduction

Malpractice suits for the management of femur and tibia fractures are frequent and expensive. Femur fracture ranks first on the list of most frequent and third on the list of most expensive suits by diagnosis. Technical problems in femur fracture management were listed as the cause of suits five times more frequently than the next three causes (i.e., failure to diagnose, infection, death).

Diagnosis/Procedure

1. Fractures about the hip and femoral shaft in children produce the most expensive judgments. The number of cases of skin necrosis, foot drop, compartment syndrome, and persistent fracture deformity led one reviewer to ask, "is it possible that with all the technology available today orthopaedists are forgetting the basic principles of fracture care?" Closed management of these fractures requires close observation by medical personnel and immediate intervention for complications. This type of treatment demands a high degree of skill and adherence to sound orthopaedic principles.

2. A thorough discussion with the patient (or family, in the case of children) concerning the nature of the injury and proposed treatment, the alternatives available, possible complications and their consequences, and realistic expectations must occur pre-operatively. Technical problems were frequent and expensive in the claims reviewed. This discussion is critical, because patient anger and informed consent issues are consistently noted in cases in which patients brought lawsuits. Be aware of and review all pre-operative consultations and tests (laboratory, x-ray, cardiac).

3. Internal fixation devices must be selected and used in accordance with manufacturers' printed specifications and published data from texts and professional literature.

4. Postoperative management of open fractures, or following open treatment, must include careful monitoring for possible infection. When in doubt, or in the face of established infection, obtain early consultation with an infectious disease expert.

5. Be certain of complete bone union before hardware removal. Look at x-rays yourself and don't rely on someone else's assessment of complete healing.

6. The primary care physician should be consulted early for the elderly patient, as complications occur quickly and may be irreversible.

Femoral Neck & Intertrochanteric Fractures

Complications

♦ Failure to diagnose

♦ Poor surgical performance (technical error)

♦ Loss of internal fixation

♦ Nonunion

♦ Infection

♦ Osteonecrosis

♦ Traumatic episode (falls, body contusions from imaging equipment) during treatment

♦ Wrong site surgery

Introduction

These are common fractures in the adult/elderly population and are relatively rare in growing children and young adults. They are usually the result of high velocity or severe trauma in the younger group. Significant injuries to other organ systems must be ruled out before definitive orthopaedic surgery is performed. For adult/elderly patients the trauma is usually less severe but the patient more fragile. Thus consultation as a rule should be obtained from a qualified primary care physician (or specialist when indicated) prior to surgical treatment. Serious medical complications occur rapidly, both preoperatively and post-operatively, and this risk should be discussed with patients and families as the treatment plan is developing.

Diagnosis Procedure

Failure to diagnose: Good quality radiographs are essential for diagnosis of a suspected hip fracture. Usually only an AP view is reasonably available, but a CT scan or MRI should be used if symptoms warrant further "clearance." Femoral fractures at more distal levels can be distracting and cause hip fractures, especially undisplaced ones, to be overlooked. A good general plan is to get radiographs of the entire femur before surgery and, in addition, to scan the hip area with the portable radiographic image intensifier (c-arm) before completing surgical procedures on femoral fractures elsewhere. Patients with persistent groin pain or anterior thigh and knee pain deserve extra diagnostic attention, especially when the pain is accompanied by osteopenia or other conditions that place these patients "at risk" for hip fractures.

Poor surgical performance (technical errors): Internal fixation devices must be selected and used in accordance with manufacturers' printed specifications and published data from texts and professional literature. There is no substitute for surgical skill and experience. Accepting an incomplete, inadequate, or objectively unacceptable reduction or internal fixation for whatever reason leaves the surgeon in a position that demands explanation for the patient, family, etc. A reasonable plan for managing problems should be presented promptly, including plans for "immediate" re-operation and revision and recommendations for a significant change in treatment plan. For example: "What we have is the best I could do, but I believe it has little or no chance to heal with a satisfactory result. Therefore, if the patient's general medical condition is satisfactory for surgery, we should go ahead and do a hip replacement." "Grey areas" will exist and should be discussed with the patient as to whether a "wait and see" approach is appropriate. Technical errors will not go away and will be permanently visible in the medical record. Surgeons are not perfect or super-human and should not ignore or try to hide obvious problems. Patients can be immensely understanding if they are dealt with honestly and get an explanation early so that a poor result does not suddenly become apparent without previous warning.

In general, a positive or aggressive approach to appropriate medical treatment by the original surgeon should yield the most satisfactory result.

Loss of internal fixation: This includes loss of reduction as a result of loss of fixation. This problem can occur at any time after surgery before bony union. An explanation with an appropriate search for a cause is in order. If reasonable, it should be discussed with the patient and family and a treatment plan should be presented. This plan should include discussion of repeat internal fixation vs arthroplasty. Many factors other than surgical performance may be responsible for loss of fixation; a routine admission of liability by the surgeon is not appropriate.

Nonunion: Unless there is obvious deformity of the major bone fragments, a CT scan frequently is necessary to confirm the diagnosis of nonunion. Preoperative and postoperative discussions of expected rates of nonunion in regard to location of the fracture, neck or intertrochanteric, are extremely valuable. The general principle is to avoid surprises. Certainly when nonunion can be expected to occur with a predictable frequency, the patient and family should be informed. Again, the surgeon should have a prompt plan to remedy the problem and suggest an appropriate time or situation when further treatment might be indicated. It is usually better if the treating surgeon volunteers this information first, rather than having an outside consultant make treatment recommendations.

Infection: Because most patients and families are aware that an infection can occur after any surgery, preoperative discussion is relatively noncontroversial but still essential. Many of the liability problems with infections arise from delay in diagnosis or lack of attention to signs and symptoms suggesting infection. Another problem is actual or perceived lack of concern or attention by the surgeon. Consultation with an infectious disease specialist is wise and important, but does not replace personal attention and concern by the surgeon.

Infection is a well-documented risk and in itself usually is overshadowed by problems with diagnosis or treatment. In addition to the infectious disease specialist, consultation with another orthopaedic surgeon may be valuable if special knowledge or experience is available.

Osteonecrosis: Pre-treatment discussion of osteonecrosis (ON) is important for patients with femoral neck fractures because of the documented frequency of this complication and the variations in time elapsed before the diagnosis can be confirmed. With intertrochanteric fractures, the relatively low frequency of ON should be mentioned for educational value. For patients with femoral neck fractures, clinical and radiographic follow-up of several years is necessary. Reassurance that adequate and acceptable reconstructive surgery is available may limit anxiety. It should be emphasized before treatment that ON occurs in a significant proportion of patients even with the best treatment modalities for femoral neck fractures.

Traumatic episode: Hip fracture tables and heavy overhead imaging equipment are hazards for patients. Careful attention to securing the equipment and the patient can't be overemphasized. Injuries from falls in the operating room or from C-arms forcefully striking body parts are not an expected consequence of treatment of hip fractures.

Wrong site surgery: The "sign your site" protocol used routinely should minimize this problem. There is no explanation that can excuse this mishap other than "human error" on somebody's part. The "sign your site" system is the vehicle to risk management of wrong site surgery. With femoral and intertrochanteric fractures, modern imaging should make this a very infrequent occurrence. If the operation is partially or totally completed before the mistake is recognized, and the medical status of the patient is still satisfactory, the surgeon should do the operation that was planned. The patient and family should be notified that a mistake was made and corrected as far as possible. If the mistake is recognized after leaving the operating room, the patient and family should be informed immediately and a plan for doing the procedure on the correct side should be outlined.

Tibia Fractures

Complications

Malunion/nonunion, skin problems, infections, vascular problems, pulmonary or fat embolus, and leg-length discrepancy.

Introduction

Treatment of tibia fractures ranks second on the lists of most frequent and most expensive suits by diagnosis. Nonunion or malunion of tibia fractures was the most common cause of suit, and most of these fractures involved the tibial plateau. The most expensive suits involved vascular and compartment syndrome problems.

Patient anger was present in a high percentage of claims (e.g., perceived lack of communication, billing problems, lack of informed consent). Physician peer criticism of medical care provided was noted in suits when comments were misunderstood or taken out of context.

Diagnosis/Procedures

1. Suits associated with treatment of tibial fractures are frequent and expensive. In the cases reviewed, there appeared to be less risk associated with open treatment cases than with closed reduction or external fixation cases.

2. The informed consent process must include discussions of specific risks and outcomes such as malalignment, leg-length discrepancy, nonunion, infection, and skin loss. Patient anger appeared especially focused on the "surprise" of experiencing one of these unexpected complications.

3. Reduction and fixation of tibial fractures must be adequate, as failure of or inadequate fixation often resulted in a lawsuit.

4. Postoperative care must include careful, professional observation of such problems as infection, circulatory/neurologic impairment, and skin problems. Vascular and compartment syndromes involved the largest indemnity payments. Early recognition, prompt treatment, and careful documentation of complications in the medical record are invaluable aids in defense against future claims. Obtain early consultation as appropriate with infectious disease or vascular experts.

5. There is an inordinately high incidence of problems associated with tibial plateau fractures. Therefore, these must be followed carefully, especially with regard to loss of position/malunion.

6. Document all bruised or injured skin that could lead to skin loss.

7. Be aware that the cast saw may build up heat that could damage skin.

Spine Surgery

Complications

Nerve injury, wrong level/site, failure to improve, infection, vascular injury, death.

Introduction

According to PIAA data, claims arising from spine surgery are the most expensive to defend, and have the highest average indemnity payments of all orthopaedic claims. There is a strong positive correlation between the severity of residual disability and amount of payment. A jury has real empathy for a young person in a wheelchair who testifies that he did not understand that spine surgery could result in paralysis.

Diagnosis/Procedure

Closed claims studies suggest that preoperative planning can lower the incidence of claims. Patients who have pending litigation are angry, have had multiple procedures, or who have chronic pain or a large functional component have a higher incidence of claims. Claims were more successful in cases where there was no clear correlation between physical findings and objective changes on images. Part of the informed consent should include careful counseling regarding the amount of pain relief that can be realistically expected. Patients who anticipate more than the surgeon can deliver tend to be litigious.

For fusion candidates, the patients should be informed about the advantages, risks, and FDA status of the spinal system to be used, and the discussion between the surgeon and patient should be documented.

Intraoperatively, careful positioning and padding to prevent neuropathies, pressure sores, and blindness is vital. The importance of this needs to be shared with the anesthesiologist. Periodic checking of the eyes, elbows, and slight turning of the head can be a real help to prevent pressure problems.

Intraoperative x-ray or portable radiographic image intensifier (c-arm) to confirm the correct operative level is imperative. Suits for operating on the wrong level or wrong side usually result in large indemnity payments. This is one risk that can be absolutely prevented by the surgeon. The surgeon should read his own imaging studies and correlate the preoperative level of pathology with the intraoperative film used to confirm the correct level. It is easy to miss unrecognized variations of spinal anatomy. In a patient with an acute neck injury, caution must be exercised in the use of cervical spine flexion-extension radiographs.

Technical errors are often alleged in claims against the "occasional" spine surgeon. Careful handling of soft tissues and sharp instruments around neurological structures minimizes this risk. Prolonged and forceful incisional retraction can result in postoperative wound complications.

The most common cause precipitating a claim is simply failure to improve. When a patient does not improve, the outcome can often only be successfully defended if the patient has been fully informed of the risks inherent in the procedure.

However, when there is a combination of complications, the presence of permanent impairment increases the likelihood of an indemnity payment even if the surgeon met the "standard of care."

Anger is a major ingredient along with failure to improve as the major cause of a claim. Expected complications are minimized by early recognition and timely treatment. Denying the presence of complications results in a higher incidence of claims. If a complication occurs, or if the patient fails to improve following surgery, consider follow-up tests or referring the patient for another opinion. Apparent frustration on the part of the surgeon can lead to anger on the part of the patient. By going out of your way to empathize, your rapport may help mitigate potential litigations.

Finally, studies also show that claims vary in number and magnitude of malpractice payouts when comparisons are made between different parts of the country.

Over 50% of reported incidences to malpractice carriers result in a lawsuit. Of the complications listed, nerve injury is the most common, with 80% of reported claims resulting in a suit. Complications associated with neurologic loss may be minimized by concurrent monitoring of the spinal cord with either motor or sensory evoked potentials, and/or the Stagnera wake-up test.

When a patient sues, indications for surgery were challenged in over half of the cases studied. All phases of treatment should therefore be well thought out and documented. The consent process and medical record should clearly outline the reasons for surgical intervention, and the patient and surgeon should have a full discussion about the recommended course of treatment, the alternatives, risks, and benefits.

Treatment protocols in spine surgery vary widely among practitioners. Each surgeon may have built-in biases depending on their experience and training. It is therefore helpful for physicians to be aware of various algorithms on low back pain and use them as guides for surgical decision making. Any deviation should be supported with meticulous documentation. Surgeons should also be familiar with the broad spectrum of treatment choices, indications, and confirmatory tests that cause them to recommend a particular course of treatment. Claims reviewed demonstrated a pattern of a lack of objective physical findings at the preoperative examination and a lack of correlation between physical findings and the level and extent of disease found on preoperative imaging studies.

By remaining your patient's advocate, the chance of a suit arising from a bad outcome or complication will be diminished.

Knee Arthroscopy

Complications

Infection, thrombophlebitis, surgery on wrong knee, broken instruments, nerve or vessel injury.

Introduction

In a single generation, arthroscopy has catapulted from an operation virtually unknown to the most frequently performed orthopaedic procedure. At the present rate, it is estimated that one in every three U.S. citizens will experience an arthroscopy during his/her lifetime. Fortunately, it has remained a relatively low-risk endeavor both as to frequency and expense of malpractice claims, but some common pitfalls have been identified.

Diagnosis/Procedure

1. Claims regarding postoperative complications such as infection or thrombophlebitis are usually defensible as recognized risks of procedures, risks which may occur in the absence of malpractice. Most claims will therefore allege unreasonable delay in recognition, diagnosis, and treatment of the complication. An aggressive approach toward postoperative complications will usually constitute an effective defense.

2. Arthroscopy of the knee has, compared to other orthopaedic operations, a relatively high incidence of wrong site (usually wrong side) surgery. If followed, the procedures outlined in the AAOS position on wrong site surgery, included in this text, should substantially alleviate this distressing event. For the decade ending in 1993, wrong site arthroscopy occurred approximately once in every 7,400 procedures; the indemnity at that time was surprisingly small, averaging approximately $20,000.

3. Broken instruments were commonly cited in the claims filed, but they rarely resulted in indemnity payments. Such payments made for these types of claims were usually only a few thousand dollars, typically made by the hospital or instrument maker.

4. The only large indemnity payments ($75,000 and up between 1983-1993, equivalent to approximately $100,000 and up today) resulting from arthroscopy of the knee were those involving injury to nerves or blood vessels. The nerve injuries were often due to the relatively unrefined techniques of meniscal repair of that era, although some were of no apparent cause; tourniquet time or pressure regulation was suspected. The blood vessel injuries were usually technical errors involving blind resections in the posterior compartments.

In summary, to avoid substantially all of the malpractice risk associated with knee arthroscopy, aggressively identify and manage postoperative complications, observe the AAOS position and guidelines on wrong-site surgery, and dissect carefully and always under direct vision, making another portal if necessary, in the posterior compartments.

Foot and Ankle

Complications

Malunion/nonunion, skin problems, infection, failure to diagnose, vascular compromise, nerve injury, wrong site surgery, posttraumatic arthritis, recurrent deformity.

Introduction

One hundred forty-four closed malpractice claims, involving both traumatic and nontraumatic diagnoses such as bunions, hammertoes, and diabetic foot problems were studied. Of the 144 claims, 51 (35%) resulted in indemnity payments to the plaintiff totaling $4.5 million, with an average payment of $90,000. The average defense cost was $15,000 per claim. In the opinion of the reviewers, one-third of the paid claims were determined to involve true deviation from an acceptable standard of care.

Average indemnity payments were 50% higher in cases of ankle fracture than in all others in this group. The ankle fracture cases involved more catastrophic complications, including deaths from pulmonary embolism (PE) and vascular complications resulting in amputation.

Retaliatory claims were filed by litigious patients in response to collection efforts. Use good judgment. Review charts before sending for collection.

Diagnosis/Procedure

1. Reduction and fixation of ankle fractures must be technically adequate. The majority of ankle fracture claims alleged poor surgical performance.

2. Posttraumatic arthritis can be a devastating complication after ankle fracture. The patient should be informed of the seriousness of this risk in a preoperative informed consent discussion, particularly in pylon fractures. Many of these injuries occurred in young, physically active individuals. An ankle fusion may be the only salvage. High indemnity costs were seen in this group of claims.

3. Don't leave the ankle dislocated or significantly subluxed if surgery is delayed. This can result in skin sloughs or conversion to open fracture.

4. Four fatal pulmonary emboli were encountered in our series. Consider deep venous thrombosis (DVT) prophylaxis in patients with prior history of DVT or those who require prolonged bed rest due to bilateral injuries.

5. Complaints under casts should be attended to!

6. If surgery is delayed for any reason, stabilize tissues appropriately. Avoid incisions through compromised tissue. The infections seen in this series were mainly due to skin sloughs.

7. Evaluate the arterial vascular status of patients presenting with nail pain or difficulties. Nail pain may be dysvascular in nature. Loss of a toe or limb may follow if treated inappropriately.

8. Wrong site surgery was seen. Not just the correct side but the correct site should be signed. Mistakes included wrong hammertoe, wrong interspace for Morton's neuroma, and bunion instead of bunionette correction.

9. Inform patients that limbs will be shorter after ankle or subtalar arthrodesis.

10. Obtain additional x-ray views or CT studies if subtle fractures of the foot are suspected. Common missed diagnoses were Lisfranc injuries, anterior calcaneal process fractures, and lateral talar process fractures. Stress views or CT scans may be needed to adequately evaluate Lisfranc injuries.

11. If an ankle sprain is not progressing as expected, consider MRI to exclude talar dome osteochondral injury.

12. Tourniquets should be calibrated and properly maintained.

General

1. Carefully document medical status at time of work release. Avoid allegation of premature return to work.

2. If hardware obscures the area that needs to be seen, get oblique x-rays or CT to answer the question.

3. Teenagers and alcoholics often cannot be trusted to be nonweightbearing. Adjust your treatment accordingly.

4. Adhere to the standard of care regarding the timely treatment of open injuries.

5. In addition to giving cast instructions, chart that you gave them!

6. If you testify as a non-party in a legal proceeding, do not assume you are immune from liability exposure. If you are found a non-party at fault, you may have opened yourself to a counterclaim not from the patient, but from the party being sued by the patient. Be factual in your testimony and do not make assumptions.

7. In the case of open injuries involving immersion (either marine or fresh water), treat with antibiotics specific for water-born pathogens. These organisms (vibrio and aeromonas) can produce a fulminant necrotizing process leading to amputation or circulatory collapse and death. Cephalosporins are not adequate treatment. A fluoroquinolone or aminoglycoside must be added to cover these organisms. Consider that an infectious disease consultant may be needed in these difficult cases.

Shoulder

Complications

Missed posterior shoulder dislocation often resulting from seizure; pin migration; radial nerve injury if medullary reamer penetrates the humeral shaft; sciatic nerve pressure subsequent to beach chair position.

Introduction

Technical complexities are not the problem. It's the little things that get us, such as not doing a complete examination, overlooking the x-ray report that fails to describe the lesion for which the surgeon is operating, or failing to spot the early signs of reflex sympathetic dystrophy (RSD).

Diagnosis/Procedure

1. Shoulder pain comes from many sources. Do a full evaluation. A negative shoulder arthrogram does not rule out a rotator cuff tear.

2. Four-part humeral head fractures can be surgically challenging. Get help if you are not skilled in managing these.

3. Bend pins to reduce migration; follow pin location closely postoperatively.

4. Informed consent pointers: be sure the patient is informed that subacromial decompression may include the inferior portion of acromioclavicular joint. In "snapping scapular surgery," be sure the patient understands that the outcome is unpredictable. Image conscious individuals, such as body-builders, can be sensitive to shoulder appearance, especially surgical scars and the bump of an AC separation.

5. An x-ray report that fails to describe the lesion for which you plan to operate must be amended to describe the lesion. Plaintiff's attorney can allege unnecessary surgery was performed when the report fails to describe the lesion. The operating physician's position may be defensible if the surgeon still has the original x-rays.

6. Frozen shoulder can have an associated rotator cuff tear. Document this before manipulation so that the manipulator is not blamed for the tear.

7. Reflex sympathetic dystrophy, even when the result is poor, is a defensible complication if diagnosis is established early and appropriate treatment begins promptly.

Pediatric Orthopaedics

Age Range

Birth to 18

Complications

Wrong site surgery, cast saw wounds, reliance on inadequate intraoperative x-rays, failure to supervise house staff and technical assistants, failure to have appropriate instruments at surgery, treating postoperative complaints with wishful thinking rather than aggressive reevaluation.

Introduction

A total of 180 claims filed against orthopaedists on behalf of pediatric patients were studied. Because they were not limited to anatomic area or procedure as in other studies, there was a wide range of causes of action, and interesting findings.

Diagnosis/Procedure

Spine: X-ray spine in polytrauma, if there are any complaints. Fractures are being missed at initial evaluation.

Surgery for scoliotic curves in neurofibromatosis carries a variety of increased risks.

Elbow: Do not accept deformities in supracondylar fractures.

Forearm: X-ray both ends of the bones in fractures to avoid missing Monteggia and Malgaigne lesions.

Document parental consent if cosmetic deformity must be accepted in minors.

Lower Extremity General: Peroneal nerve palsies, ulcers as a result of casts or skin traction, and cast saw injuries resulted in surprisingly high indemnity payments. Bryant's traction improperly done resulted in a number of claims because of skin ulcers and/or foot drop.

Allowing teenagers early weightbearing is a risky business. We saw good fracture reductions destroyed (internally fixed or in cast) when teenagers were allowed weightbearing too early.

When hardware is being removed account for each piece. If in doubt, x-ray the site before closing.

Hip/Thigh: Follow questionable congenital dislocation of the hip for a long time.

Knee: Have objective findings in teenage girls with knee pain before arthroscopy.

Leg: The peroneal nerve is a "structure at risk." It is exposed to injury whether treatment is surgery, cast, or traction. It should be treated with respect.

Ehler Danlos: Get a pre-op pediatric consult. Some varieties of this disease are associated with weak mitral valves and arterial wall insufficiency, posing anesthesia risks.

Pearls

Casts: There is no such thing as a hypochondriac in a cast; listen to complaints. Cast saw wounds are common. Supervise assistants. Dull saws generate enough heat to burn skin.

When a plaster cast gets wet and then dries, the padding sticks to the plaster. The padding then loses its ability to protect the skin from the saw.

Avoid Wrong Site Surgery: Mark the skin of the operative site at the pre-op area when a parent is present, according to the AAOS Position on Wrong Site Surgery.

Intraoperative x-rays should be used liberally to identify specific sites.

Total Joint

Complications

The known complications of total hip arthroplasty include neuropathy, leg-length discrepancy, infection, technical failure due to malposition, instrument failure, and dislocation. Also, there were miscellaneous vascular injuries and complaints of persistent pain. Other complications were those of pulmonary embolism and trochanteric nonunion.

Introduction

Operative procedures on joint structures (exclusive of spinal fusion) are interventions that result in the most claims against orthopaedic surgeons. This was true in 1998 and also in the cumulative data from January 1, 1985 to December 31, 1998. Of the 14,979 orthopaedic surgery claims which were closed between 1985 and 1998, 23.7% involved operative procedures on joint structures (the PIAA report did not differentiate the various categories). Almost 29% were paid on behalf of orthopaedic surgeons involving joint procedures. As a comparison, 11.7% of claims and 7.6% of indemnity were for the next most prevalent category of claims, the group that included diagnostic interview, evaluation, or consultation ("failure to diagnose").

The most prevalent allegation of medical misadventure in orthopaedic surgery was improper performance, which was reported as the primary issue in 39.4% of claims reported between 1985 and 1998. For most claims in 1998 alone, improper performance was again the primary cause for a malpractice suit and was reported in 47.2% of claims. Moreover, in 52% of claims paid in 1998, improper performance was the primary allegation. For claims involving improper performance, operative procedures on joint structures (exclusive of spinal fusion) were the most prevalent, and they were responsible for the highest average payment of $162,736.

Diagnosis/Procedure

1. The patient should be advised in preoperative discussions that pain may not be completely relieved. Persistence of or increased postoperative pain is one of the major causes of litigation. Although total joint arthroplasty is usually very effective for relief of discomfort, in some cases pain may be worse after surgery or may not be completely relieved.

2. The patient should be advised about the possibility of sciatic nerve injury. This played a role in over 20% of the malpractice cases. Sciatic nerve injury usually results from a stretch, and substantial recovery usually occurs within the first year.

3. Postoperative leg length inequality causes patient dissatisfaction, particularly when associated with pain. Lengthening of the operated side caused the most distress and resulted in some malpractice actions.

4. Major vascular injury produced death in 6% of the cases. Inadvertent vessel injury was often associated with reamers or other sharp instruments which were placed through the pelvis. It is therefore paramount that this type of complication be diagnosed immediately, and definitive action taken. Detailed knowledge of osseous anatomy and the location of intra-pelvic structures helps avoid this complication, particularly in revision procedures or in atypical cases.

5. Templates and sizing films should be referred to, and old records obtained and consulted before surgery is attempted. Reliance on the advice of the manufacturer's representative is inadvisable.

6. Recurrent postoperative dislocations often result in one or more revisions and are a significant cause of litigation. This problem is often associated with the malposition of components.

7. It is important to be aware of patients who are apt to engage in risky behavior or substance abuse.

8. Suspected total joint infections must be considered without hesitation on the part of the operating surgeon. Prompt and definitive action should be taken immediately and usually includes a consultation with the infectious disease department.

9. The best risk management includes a thorough discussion with the patient and the family, with a detailed informed consent component.

10. Failure to recognize postoperative infections in total knee arthroplasty cases in a timely manner was the cause of many suits.

In Summary

A detailed informed consent discussion with each patient must occur with the specific mention of the possibility of infection. There should be specific discussions of other possible complications, such as loosening, deep vein thrombosis and/or pulmonary embolism, as well as possible injury to nerves and vessels. Mechanical failures such as prosthetic wear and breakage should be mentioned. Postoperatively, one should think the worst and act quickly. Denial is the enemy of rational intervention, often resulting in severe problems for the patient and resultant litigation.

Appendices

Principles of Office Practice Management

These principles are presented with an eye toward minimizing exposure to liability risk in the office setting. They should be considered as suggestions only and are not representative of any formal policies of the Academy nor as guidelines which must be adhered to by the orthopaedist.

Injections and Aspirations

Common sense governs most elements of this category, but as reminders of special considerations:

1. **Medication History.** Drug allergies and untoward adverse reactions to medicines should be queried prior to injection, and **known allergies and drug reactions should be on prominent display in the medical record** (preferably on page one of the paper or electronic medical record).

2. **Infection Control.** In addition to careful adherence to principles of sterile technique, both federal law and most state laws dictate specific methods of disposal of medical waste. Familiarize yourself with the OSHA Regulations on Bloodborne Pathogens and other related regulations and laws.

3. **Observation.** After receiving injections, patients must be observed for reactions to the injectables, and a "crash cart" or its equivalent must be readily accessible and its whereabouts known to all office employees.

4. **Records.** Keep an accurate record of medication name, dosage, site injected and any observed reactions.

Casts

Studies have shown that most litigation arising from cast problems results from casts applied hastily or by inadequately trained personnel. Be sure that those in the office who do apply casts are properly trained, and watch for excessive heat generation in the freshly applied cast. Cast cutters continue to injure patients, so develop the skills required to take off casts without cutting or burning the patient. The patient should be given written instructions on care of the cast at home, and appropriate arrangements made regarding follow-up. The orthopaedist should never ignore complaints of problems with a cast.

Office Radiography

A few reminders regarding the office radiography suite:

1. **Women.** Inquire regarding possible pregnancy, and shield appropriately.

2. **Personnel and Equipment.** Most states have regulations which address both your radiographic equipment and the technicians who operate it. Familiarize yourself with these requirements, and request an inspection by the state if that is appropriate in your locale.

3. **Safety.** All personnel exposed to radiation in the office must wear proper badges to monitor that exposure, and these must be checked on a regular basis to track their cumulative exposure.

Outpatient Surgical Procedures

Whether done in a hospital outpatient surgical suite, free-standing surgery center or office surgical suite, outpatient procedure records should include at least the following:

1. Pre-op diagnosis and history and physical completed and in the medical record prior to the procedure.

2. Appropriate lab and other diagnostic materials also present in or with the medical record.

3. Documentation in the record of an informed consent discussion with the patient and/or family member.

4. A formal operative report completed in timely fashion postoperatively, with a copy to the office record.

5. Attention to wrong-site surgery is just as important in outpatients as in the inpatient setting. Sign Your Site.

Selection of procedures to be done in the office surgical suite must be done carefully, especially as it is difficult to find expert witness support for procedures deemed after the fact to be "too lengthy or too complex" for the office setting, thereby posing difficulties in defense of a claim should an adverse outcome result.

Office Procedures/Issues

Many aspects of office operations have direct and subtle impact on the orthopaedist's exposure to claims. Several of these include:

1. **Telephones.** This is the first contact with your office, and it should be prompt, pleasant, informed and helpful. This is the time at which the tone of your relationship with a patient is first set, and will influence his/her response to events which occur in the course of treatment.

2. **Appointments.** The office with the happiest patients is that which sets a realistic appointment schedule, then meets that schedule without long patient waiting times.

3. **Billing/Insurance.** Informed office personnel must explain to patients the elements of your charges; the benefits available from third party payers; deductibles and co-pays on their coverage; and any other insurance issues. No patient should be "surprised" by receipt of your bill for care.

4. **Medications/Refills.** Explain to patients your procedures for refills both during and after office hours. Maintain simple records of refills or new prescriptions, wherever provided, to include samples given in the office. In addition, care should be exercised with custody of your blank prescriptions, and pre-signed blanks are to be avoided for obvious reasons.

5. **Medical Records.** While the actual record belongs to the physician, the information therein is the patient's property; do not hesitate to provide a patient with a copy of the record. Establish a routine mechanism for notifying referring physicians of your findings and recommendations. Clinical records must be timely prepared, contain no retroactive additions or corrections, and must be complete and legible — preferably typed. Paper records regarding formal complaints or disciplinary actions, peer review or other such proceedings should be maintained in a

separate file established for such information.

6. **Laboratory Data.** Establish an office routine such that all reports of laboratory or other diagnostic examination are seen by the physician, initialed or otherwise marked to document that it has been reviewed, followup arranged with the patient if that is appropriate, and filed in the medical record after completing the steps noted above.

7. **"Patient Abandonment."** If you find it necessary to discharge a patient from your care, have an established procedure to do so, and follow it in every instance. One physician insurer suggests: notification via certified mail with return receipt; an offer to provide copies of records in your possession; and noting that you will be available for true emergencies only until a time certain, perhaps 30 days from the date of the letter. Be aware that federal EMTALA regulations strictly govern the transfer of patients who are acutely ill or injured. Do not get into a paper "joust" with a patient you will no longer care for.

Emergency Department Coverage Issues

Two categories of events related to the emergency department have produced an increased number of claims against orthopaedists in recent years:

1. **Inadequate Information.** When evaluating a call from an emergency physician regarding a patient, either new or established, be sure you understand the abilities of the calling physician to have done a complete evaluation and to describe accurately the historical, clinical, and laboratory findings. If doubt remains, the prudent course of action is to evaluate the patient's problem personally and not rely on questionable information presented on the telephone.

2. **Coverage Confusion.** Establish clearly with the emergency department that you are or are not accepting referrals. This is especially true with groups in which some of the physicians accept referrals and others do not. Patients are frustrated and angry to discover, hours or days after the ER visit, that the orthopaedist whose name was given is unwilling to provide subsequent care. This may be especially problematic in the event a true emergency develops in the patient after he or she leaves the ER.

Managed Care: An Overview of Specific Risk and Liability Issues

In 1995, over 151 million U.S. citizens were enrolled in managed care organizations, and this number is expected to increase. Therefore, it is important for the orthopaedist's professional liability insurance policy to provide coverage for the unique exposures.

Many professional liability policies provide coverage for "direct patient care activities only" where coverage is not provided, or is specifically excluded, for other activities in which the orthopaedist may participate such as peer review, credentialling, and quality and utilization review. However, managed care contracts may specify that the orthopaedist must participate in non-patient-care activities, but without contractual language indicating that the organization will defend or indemnify the physician against claims based upon such activities.

Because of these risks, it is important that the orthopaedist carefully review any such contract with personal legal counsel and the professional liability insurer prior to executing it. The purpose of this review is to identify potential risk and to exclude it from the contract, or to ensure that they are either indemnified by the managed care organization, or covered by the physician's professional liability insurance policy. It is not acceptable for a managed care entity to require the orthopaedist to sign a provider agreement "on the spot" without review or negotiation, as has occurred in various locales across the country.

In reviewing managed care contracts, the orthopaedist should consider the following items and seek contract additions, deletions, modifications, or indemnification agreements prior to executing the contract:

1. **Hold harmless and indemnification clauses.** Orthopaedists should not enter into any contract which specifies that they will indemnify another party in the event a claim is brought. The professional liability policy provides coverage for patient care activities by the *physician only*, and in most cases specifically excludes coverage assumed contractually by the physician for other parties, such as the managed care company. An ideal managed care contract should require only that the physician provide evidence of in-force professional liability insurance. There should be no contractual language specifying any additional liability on the part of the physician, for example, for claims made against the physician and managed care entity for denial or delay in care due to the managed care organization's gatekeeper and approval processes. Physicians have faced multi-million-dollar judgments rendered against managed care organizations for delay/denial of care, simply because the physicians have signed provider agreements that contain these hold harmless/indemnification clauses.

2. **Open communication.** Contract provisions that prohibit or discourage communication between physicians (gag clauses) and patients may preclude discussion of any disagreements regarding a plan's approved treatment guidelines, disincentives or financial incentives to provide only certain tests or other care. Patients have successfully sued physicians and managed care organizations as a result of this lack of communication. Gag clauses are now illegal in many states.

3. **Guidelines for appointment and termination.** The contract should address guidelines for appointment and termination of the physician, as well as notification to patients of the physician's termination and the patients' options.

4. **Grievance procedures.** Grievance procedures for both the physician and the patient should be spelled out, for the timely appeal of adverse decisions by the managed care organization, preferably to an objective or independent panel as has been established in several states.

5. **Procedures for transfer of insurance.** The contract should address the procedure for transferring an established patient to a new insurance plan during treatment.

6. **Physician-specific data.** The contract should disclose how such data is to be collected, how it will be used, and the ability of the physician to review and respond to the data or its interpretation prior to its release. Data should be considered and treated as confidential and not subject to discovery or used as evidence in judicial or administrative proceedings.

7. **Provisions for independent review.** Timely, independent review should be permitted and the procedures for such review spelled out when investigational or experimental treatment is denied.

8. **Confidentiality of credentials.** The credentialling process and records must be confidential; due process must be specifically described and provided; documentation requests must be reasonable both in time and quantity; and liability releases must not exceed those required by law. The physician should not be required to query the National Practitioner Data Bank on behalf of the managed care company.

9. **Mix of providers/referrals.** The plan's provider network should include an appropriate mix of high quality specialists, to permit referral of any medical condition. Ideally, the physician should be able to refer "out of network" when the provider network does not include the type of specialist the physician feels it would be in the patient's best interest to see.

10. **Approval of care/management review.** Patient management review decisions should be done by physician reviewers in the same specialty who are local or regional, rather than out of state, and should be based on published standards. Plan medical directors and reviewers should be easily available to the treating physician.

11. **Provisions for in-house procedures.** Specialty specific in-house procedures and supplies should be allowed, such as radiographs, physical therapy, minor procedures, and durable medical goods, where the provision of such care is not in conflict with federal or state law.

12. **Review of guidelines.** Clinical guidelines, protocols, and pathways used by

the plan should be available for review by the physician prior to executing a contract.

13. **Incentives.** Financial incentives to control cost create a conflict of interest for the physician and in some states are illegal. If the financial incentive is set too high the physician works for the managed care organization rather than the patient.

14. **Provider contract charges.** The provider agreement should specify that both the physician and the managed care organization must agree, in writing, to changes in the provider agreement, including reimbursement, incentives, and appeal mechanisms. Many managed care organization contracts specify that the entity may unilaterally change the provider agreement, even despite protest by the physician provider.

The physician's primary interest is to deliver the highest quality of care in a stable doctor-patient relationship. This may conflict with the managed care organization's goal of controlling costs through primary care gatekeepers, avoiding inpatient hospital care, limiting referral, and using various layers of bureaucratic decision making required for treatment processes.

The orthopaedist's best protection against the liabilities inherent in a managed care environment is to continue to be the patient's advocate for the highest quality of care available. If a managed care organization denies what the physician considers to be appropriate care, it is the responsibility of the physician to exhaust all appeal mechanisms on behalf of the patient. Records should reflect that the physician has discussed with the patient any actions with which the physician disagrees and the potential results. These discussions may be related to delay or failure to approve testing, treatment, continuing inpatient care, or referral.

Malpractice Risks Related to Telemedicine

Traditionally, telemedicine was limited to readings of radiographs or pathologic slides sent via mail and an occasional telephone consultation between colleagues. However, with expansion of telecommunications capabilities, new opportunities for practicing medicine at a distance have emerged. These include a variety of formats, up to full real-time two-way video and audio.

One consideration is *venue*. If the encounter occurs across state lines, whose laws govern? Many states do not address this question but those that do who usually place control in the state where the patient is located. This means that if a malpractice claim ensues the physician may have to defend in a distant locale with the attendant expense, inconvenience, and possible legal disadvantage.

Another consideration is *licensure*. All states require persons who practice medicine within their borders to be licensed to do so, except under a few very specific and infrequent circumstances such as emergencies and "collegial consultations." There is currently a discussion in many state legislatures and to some extent at the federal level regarding whether special limited licenses (as recommended by the Federation of State Medical Boards) or full license (advocated by the AMA and American College of Radiology) shall be required for the practice of telemedicine. Either way, if a malpractice claim results from a medical encounter across state lines and the physician is not

licensed in the state where the patient resides, the physician may be found liable for the unauthorized practice of medicine. It should be noted that most malpractice insurance policies do not require the insurance company to defend the physician in such circumstances or to pay the judgment, if there is one.

A third risk is *malpractice coverage*. Even if the physician is properly licensed, will he or she be covered for claims arising from telemedicine? At the present time, there are no documented cases of refusal, and most companies do not ask applicants whether telemedicine is part of the practice. However, it seems likely that more will do so if claims become frequent and possibly impose a surcharge for the coverage.

The fourth issue is *confidentiality*. Protection of electronically stored medical records from hackers or just curious accessors may be difficult and the physician is likely to be held accountable even if not directly responsible for the system's security.

The fifth issue is *informed consent:* how obtained, recorded, archived, and by whom. Does the fact that the encounter takes place over a distance, of itself, require an additional consent in addition to consent for the medical encounter?

Finally, it is not always clear at what point a physician-patient relationship has been established, which is a crucial point if a malpractice claim should ensue. There are 50 different answers but some generalities may be drawn. In some states simply "holding one's self out as a practitioner" in a clinical setting is sufficient, including the use of "M.D." or any similar appellation. In most states laws refer to one who "diagnoses or treats" or "attempts to diagnose or treat," leaving the definition of those words to the courts. It is easy to imagine situations where the physician will not consider himself/herself to have practiced medicine, such as informal discussion in "chat rooms," but the patient will. In most of these, the law seems to be on the side of the patient. A disclaimer by the physician is not likely to be an effective shield. If his/her actions constitute the practice of medicine, according to the laws of the state in question, most courts will probably rule that the physician has practiced medicine, any disclaimer to the contrary notwithstanding. Also, failure to send a bill for services is unlikely to be a defense against having practiced medicine, although sending one will almost certainly establish that the physician did so or at least thought he/she did.

Wrong-Site Surgery

Wrong-site surgery is a devastating problem that affects both the patient and surgeon and results from poor preoperative planning, lack of institutional controls, failure of the surgeon to exercise due care, or a simple mistake in communication between the patient and the surgeon.

Wrong-site surgery is not just an orthopaedic surgery problem that occurs because the surgeon operates on the wrong limb. This is a system problem that affects other surgical specialties as well. While the number of reported orthopaedic surgery cases is not high relative to the total number of orthopaedic professional liability insurance claims, a retrospective study of a sample of insurers across the country provides evidence, over a ten-year period, that 84% of the cases involving wrong-site orthopaedic surgery claims resulted in indemnity payments, compared to all other types of orthopaedic surgery claims in which indemnity payments were made in only 30% of orthopaedic surgery claims during this same time period.

Recommendations for Eliminating Wrong-Site Surgery

Although the wrong-site surgery problem has been addressed on a local level in many areas of the country, there has been no organized national effort to eliminate wrong-site surgery. The Canadian Orthopaedic Association mounted a significant educational program from 1994 to 1996 to eliminate this problem and has reported that the number of known wrong-site orthopaedic surgery claims in Canada has subsequently dropped dramatically.

The American Academy of Orthopaedic Surgeons believes that a unified effort among surgeons, hospitals and other health care providers to initiate preoperative and other institutional regulations can effectively eliminate wrong-site surgery in the United States.

Consequently, the AAOS urges other surgical and health care provider groups to join the effort in implementing effective controls to eliminate this problem.

Effective Methods of Eliminating Wrong-Site Surgery

Wrong-site surgery is preventable by having the surgeon's initials placed on the operative site using a permanent marking pen and then operating through or adjacent to his or her initials. Spinal surgery done at the wrong level can be prevented with an intraoperative x-ray that marks the exact vertebral level (site) of surgery. Similarly, institutional protocols should include these recommendations and involve operating room nurses and technicians, hospital room committees, anesthesiologists, residents, and other preoperative allied health personnel.

Consequently, eliminating wrong-site surgery means the surgeon's initials are placed on the operative site in a way that cannot be overlooked and in a manner that will be clearly incorrect if transferred onto another body area prior to surgery. The patient's records should also be available in the operating facility.

In keeping with its Code of Ethics, the Academy believes that in any communication with the patient or patient's family regarding care rendered—particularly in relation to an untoward event such as wrong site surgery—orthopaedic surgeons must be truthful in all circumstances.

As indicated in the attached recommendations, particular circumstances of individual cases require specific and different actions on the part of the surgeon in the event that wrong site surgery is discovered, but in all cases the patient's choice and the best interest of the patient should be the determining factors in decision making.

September, 1997

Recommendations for Management Following the Discovery of Wrong-Site Surgery

A. General

If, during the course of a surgical procedure, or after surgery has been completed, it is determined that the surgery is being or has been performed at the wrong site, the surgeon should always:

1. act in accord with the patient's best interests and to promote the patient's well-being; and

2. record the events in appropriate medical records.

B. General Anesthesia

If the procedure is being performed under general anesthesia, when it is determined that the surgery is being performed at the wrong site, the surgeon should:

1. take appropriate steps to return the patient, as nearly as possible, to the patient's preoperative condition;

2. perform the desired procedure at the correct site, unless there are medical reasons not to proceed. For example, if proceeding with the surgery at the correct site would materially increase the risk associated with extended length of the surgical procedure or if correct site surgery would likely result in an additional and unacceptable disability; and

3. advise the patient, and the patient's family, if appropriate, as soon as reasonably possible, of what occurred and the likely consequences, if any, of the wrong-site surgery.

C. Local Anesthesia

If the procedure is being performed under a local anesthesia and the patient is clearly able to comprehend what has occurred and competent to exercise judgment, the surgeon should:

1. take appropriate steps to return the patient, as nearly as possible, to the patient's preoperative condition;

2. advise the patient of what has occurred, recommend to the patient what, in the surgeon's best judgment, is the appropriate course for the patient to follow under the circumstances; and

3. truthfully answer any relevant question posed by the patient and then proceed as directed by the patient.

D. Discovery After Surgery

If, after the surgical procedure has been completed, it is determined that the surgery was performed at the wrong site, the surgeon should:

1. as soon as reasonably possible, discuss the mistake with the patient and, if appropriate, with the patient's family; and

2. recommend an immediate plan to rectify the mistake unless there is a medical reason not to proceed.

Report of the Task Force On Wrong-Site Surgery and Sample Hospital Policy for Surgical Site Identification

September 1997
Revised, February 1998

*88% of orthopaedic surgeons surveyed (12/98) either agreed or strongly agreed that the "Sign Your Site" Program would reduce the incidence of wrong-site surgery

Report of the Task Force on Wrong-Site Surgery

S. Terry Canale, MD, Chair
Secretary, American Academy of Orthopaedic Surgeons
Memphis, TN

September 1997
(Revised February 1998)

Members

Jesse DeLee, MD
Chair, Program Committee
American Academy of Orthopaedic Surgeons
San Antonio, TX

Allen Edmonson, MD
Board of Directors
State Volunteer Mutual Insurance Co.
Brentwood, TN

Steven S. Fountain, MD
Chair, Committee on Professional Liability
American Academy of Orthopaedic Surgeons
Los Gatos, CA

Andrew J. Weiland, MD
Vice Chair, Council on Education
American Academy of Orthopaedic Surgeons
New York, NY

Lori Bartholomew, Consultant
Physicians Insurers Association of America
Rockville, MD

John Thomason, JD
Counsel and Consultant
State Volunteer Mutual Insurance Co.
Memphis, TN

Kristin Olds Glavin, JD
Associate General Counsel
American Academy of Orthopaedic Surgeons
Rosemont, IL

Mark W. Wieting
Vice President, Education Programs
American Academy of Orthopaedic Surgeons
Rosemont, IL

Ex-Officio:
James D. Heckman, MD
First Vice President
American Academy of Orthopaedic Surgeons
San Antonio, TX

Richard H. Gelberman, MD
Chair, Council on Education
American Academy of Orthopaedic Surgeons
St. Louis, MO

Report of the American Academy of Orthopaedic Surgeons Task Force on Wrong-Site Surgery

September 1997
(Revised February 1998)

The charge of this task force was to determine the incidence (number of claims), mechanism, resulting disability, and method of prevention of wrong-site surgery. This task force was established by the Council on Education of the American Academy of Orthopaedic Surgeons because of recent national publicity about wrong-site surgery and because a method for preventing wrong-site surgery in orthopaedic patients is needed.

Incidence (Number of Claims)

The Physicians Insurers Association of America (PIAA), with the help of Lori Bartholomew, PIAA consultant, documented the incidence of wrong-site surgery for the years 1985 through 1995.[1] Data were accumulated from 22 member medical malpractice carriers representing 110,000 physicians. During this time, there were 225 claims for orthopaedic wrong-site surgery, compared to only 106 claims for other surgical specialties (Table 1); however, the median pay-out for wrong-site surgery was smaller for orthopaedic cases than for other surgical cases.

The average payment for all orthopaedic claims was $125,817 (Table 2), which is two and a half times the average payment for wrong-site surgery ($48,087). It is interesting to note that 84% of closed claims for wrong-site surgery resulted in payment, compared to only 30% of all other closed orthopaedic claims. Claims involving wrong-site surgery constitute only 1.8% of all orthopaedic

Table 1 Physician Insurers Association of America (PIAA) 22 Member Medical Malpractice Carriers/110,000 Physicians January 1985–December 1995

Wrong-site Claims	Number Closed	Number Paid	Percent Paid	Average* Payment	Median* Payment
Orthopaedic surgeons	225	189	84%	$48,087	$20,000
Other surgical specialties	106	72	67.9%	$76,167	$25,000

Source: Physician Insurers Association of America, Rockville, MD
*The median payment is the mid-point, and the sum of all indemnity payments divided by the number of claims that it represents is the average.

Table 2 PIAA Data, Jan. 1985–Dec. 1995

Payment (Average)	
All orthopaedic claims	$125,817
Wrong-site claims	$ 48,087
Percentage of Claims Resulting in Payment	
All orthopaedic claims	30%
Wrong-site claims	84%
Percentage of All Orthopaedic Malpractice Claims Attributable to Wrong-site Surgery	**1.8%**

Source: Physician Insurers Association of America, Rockville, MD

Table 3 State Volunteer Mutual Insurance Co. (Tennessee) 37 Medical Malpractice Claims, 1977–1997

	Range	Mean
Age		
Age of Insured Physician at Time of Surgery	33–73 yrs	46 yrs
Age of Patient at Time of Surgery	12–90 yrs	40.5 yrs
Location		
Hospital operating room	36	
Outpatient surgery center	1	

Source: State Volunteer Mutual Insurance Co., Brentwood, TN

surgery claims, indicating that orthopaedic wrong-site surgery is relatively rare.

Mechanism

With the help of the State Volunteer Mutual Insurance Company (Tennessee) (SVMIC), the American Academy of Orthopaedic Surgeons Task Force was able to obtain detailed information from 37 abstracts of wrong-site surgery claims filed in Tennessee from 1977 to 1997; 10 of these claims are still open.[2] The information taken from these abstracts, shown in Table 3, included the average age of the physicians insured at the time of surgery, the average age of the patients, and whether the surgery occurred in a hospital or outpatient surgery center. All but one of the wrong-site surgical procedures were done in a hospital operating room.

The Tennessee claims data also indicate, (Table 4):

♦ the anatomic site of the procedure

♦ the type of surgery performed

♦ the category of wrong-site surgery

In these 37 cases, wrong-site surgery was most common in arthroscopic knee proce-

dures (15), and the most common mistake was that the correct procedure was done but on the wrong (contralateral) side (29). Foot procedures (7) had the second highest frequency of wrong-site surgery.

Of the 37 cases reviewed in the SVMIC study, the discovery that surgery was taking place on the wrong site occurred during surgery in 59.5% of the cases (Table 5). Of those cases, the surgeon proceeded to do the planned surgery on the correct side during the same anesthesia in 20 out of 22 cases.

If the error was discovered after surgery, the family or responsible party was notified and the procedure was either delayed, postponed, cancelled, or performed by another surgeon (15 of 15).[2]

Because of the above findings, the Task Force has developed recommendations for management by the orthopaedist following discovery of wrong-site surgery. These recommendations are found in Appendix 1.

Disability and Loss Incurred

In most cases, the surgeon was in error or an incorrect site was prepared and draped by hospital staff. In a few cases, the patient may

Table 4 37 Medical Malpractice Cases 1977–1997

Anatomic Site of Wrong-Site Procedure — Number of Cases

Knee	15	Leg	3
Ankle/foot	9	Hand/fingers	3
Hip	5	Wrist	2

Type of Orthopaedic Surgery Performed — Number of Cases

Arthroscopy	15	Hardware removal	1
Foot procedures	7	Fracture repair	3
Hip fracture/SFCE	5	Osteotomy	1
Hand procedures	5		

Category of Wrong-Site Surgery - Number of Cases

Wrong side/correct procedure	29	Correct side/wrong finger	2
Correct site/wrong procedure	5	Correct site/wrong tendon	1

Source: State Volunteer Mutual Insurance Co., Brentwood, TN

Table 5 SVMIC Sudy: Discovery of Error

Time of Discovery of Wrong Surgery Site	Number of Cases	Percent
During surgery	22	59.5
After surgery	15	40.5
Action Upon Discovery of Error		
Immediate performance of planned surgery	20	54
Delayed/ postponed planned surgery	9	24.4
Planned surgery cancelled/ performed by other	8	21.6

Source: State Volunteer Mutual Insurance Co., Brentwood, TN

have given incorrect information or a documentation error was made either on the operative permit or on the preoperative radiographs (Table 6).

The average loss in the 27 closed claims for wrong-site surgery was $33,000, slightly less than the national average of $48,087 for wrong-site surgery in the PIAA claims database of all closed orthopaedic claims. The loss incurred was most commonly shared by the physician and the hospital (Table 7).

Most patients had no residual deficit other than a cosmetic one (26), although there were additional medical expenses. Sequelae in a few patients included impairment at the incorrect operative site (4), permanent dis-

ability (3), contracture (2), and nonunion (1) (Table 8).

During the 20 years from 1977 to 1997, an average of 251 orthopaedic surgeons were insured by State Volunteer Mutual Insurance Company. It can thus be extrapolated that the chance probability of an orthopaedist performing wrong-site surgery in a career (of 35 years) is 1 in 4.

Prevention

The literature concerning prevention of wrong-site surgery is virtually nonexistent, but some methods have been recommended.[3] A review of the recommendations of the

Table 6 SVMIC Study: Cause of Claim

Cause of Claim	Number of cases	Percent
Physician error (alone)	17	46
Incorrect site prepared/draped by hospital staff	15	40
Patient gave incorrect information about site	3	8
Documentation error on operative permit/ x-ray	2	5

Source: State Volunteer Mutual Insurance Co., Brentwood, TN

Table 7 SVMIC Study: Loss Incurred

Loss Incurred	Number of cases	Percent
Shared by M.D. and hospital	18	49
Individual for physician/ group only	9	24
Claim file remains open	10	27
Payment of closed claims (27) paid (average)	$33,000	

Source: State Volunteer Mutual Insurance Co., Brentwood, TN

Table 8 SVMIC Study: Permanent Injury

Injury - Permanent	Number of cases	Percent
None, other than cosmetic	26	70
Residual impairment at incorrect site	4	11
Permanent disability	3	8
Contracture	2	5
Nonunion	1	3
Pending	1	3

Source: State Volunteer Mutual Insurance Co., Brentwood, TN

Alamo Orthopaedic Society (Dr. James Giles), the Canadian Orthopaedic Association[4] (Dr. Paul Wright), and the MAG Mutual Insurance Company of Georgia[5] suggests a method of limb identification that is simple, reproducible, non-intimidating to the patient, and easily seen by all appropriate hospital staff and surgeons. This method requires the surgeon to use a permanent marking pen to place his or her initials on the site of surgery and then operate through or adjacent to the initials. Before surgery, the surgeon checks the patient's chart and radiographs, has the patient identify the correct site and side to be operated on, and then marks the site with his or her initials. The initials should not be draped out of the operative field, and the surgeon should not make an incision unless the initials are visible. The initials made with the permanent marking pen fade within 5 to 7 days without leaving a permanent tattoo, and making such a mark should not alter the infection rate. Statistics from the Canadian Orthopaedic Association indicate that in the past two years of using this method, the frequency of wrong-site surgery among their membership has decreased; however, these statistics may not be significant because of the small number of cases occurring each year.[6]

The simple use of an "X" to identify the correct or incorrect site or side has not been consistently successful. Also, marking the wrong leg has failed when the marked leg was draped out of the field and the surgeon was unsure as to whether the other leg was marked or not.[4]

A similar method of limb identification has been adopted elsewhere. The Task Force reviewed the abstract of an unpublished retrospective study from Dr. Douglas G. Wright, of wrong-site surgery conducted by a malpractice insurance firm and three hospitals. This study of 11 cases revealed, among other findings, that general anesthesia was used in 10 cases, the surgeon was not in the operating room for induction of anesthesia or preoperative preparation of the patient in 7 of the cases, and was frequently "rushed," and prone or lateral positioning of the patient in 5 of the 11 cases may have been a disorienting factor for the surgeon. As a result of this study, the hospitals adopted a protocol calling for the patient to mark the surgical site with indelible ink. When the patient is unable to cooperate, the surgical staff performs the task in the preoperative area before the anesthesia is administered.

Several cases have been reviewed where the patient was obtunded and an operation carried out at the wrong site because the x-ray was incorrectly labeled. If the patient cannot substantiate the correct side and the x-ray is to be used to make this determination, it is mandatory to substantiate that the x-ray is correct. Repeating the x-ray or use of an image intensifier prior to making an incision can solve this problem.

To avoid wrong-site (level) spinal surgery, the MAG Mutual Insurance Company, in its premium reduction program, recommends an intraoperative spinal radiograph to determine the exact location and level of spinal surgery.

The Task Force also obtained information from the Midwest Medical Insurance Company (MMIC), Minneapolis, Minnesota, which in February 1997 issued a Risk Management Advisory based on a MMIC task force review of 11 closed claims involving spine surgery performed at the wrong level.[7] The claims, all of which were found to be indefensible, involved 7 male and 4 female patients with an average age of 46 years. All patients had disk herniations and all surgeries were performed at a single level. In all but one case, the surgeries were performed one level higher than intended. The common cause of error was over-reliance on unreliable techniques for identifying and marking the appropriate level.

As a result, the MMIC Task Force recommended the following procedures to surgeons:

1. Review all necessary documents that indicate what levels are to be operated on.

2. Use a reliable technique to identify the level:

   ♦ Expose the lamina at the operative site

   ♦ Mark the intended level using an instrument or clip at the level of the exposed laminae

   ♦ X-ray the patient and personally interpret the x-ray

   ♦ Indelibly mark the site by cautery, stitch, or "bone bite" *before* moving the x-ray marker.

3. Work with radiologists to develop consistent "level" terminology (eg, "L3-4", not "L-3") and consistent conventions for counting and labeling vertebrae.

Education

Education should be aimed at two audiences: orthopaedists (including residents and fellows) and operating room personnel.

Orthopaedists

The methods to prevent wrong-site surgery should be disseminated to the fellowship of the American Academy of Orthopaedic Surgeons through various venues, including the annual meeting, CME courses (both skills and non-skills), slide programs, and video-tapes. A slide program and videotape should be prepared by the AAOS staff to facilitate getting this information to course chairmen as quickly as possible. An article also should be published in the *AAOS Bulletin* [published Oct. 1997]. The Council of Musculoskeletal Specialty Societies and the Board of Councilors should receive this information in a form suitable for publication in their respective newsletters or bulletins and for CME purposes. Specific education programs should be provided for all orthopaedic residency programs. Finally, an advisory statement should be prepared concerning the AAOS recommendations for preventing wrong-site surgery.

Operating Room Personnel

In some of the material reviewed, operating room personnel and anesthesiologists follow a hospital policy to administer anesthesia only after the correct extremity has been marked with the surgeon's initials. This indicates a reasonable concern for this problem by the entire surgical team. It is therefore recommended that the information on preventing wrong-site surgery be disseminated to groups involved, including operating room nurses and technicians, anesthesiologists, and hospital operating room committees.

Summary

♦ Wrong-site surgery in orthopaedics is relatively infrequent, but may have significant physical and psychological effects on both the patient and the surgeon.

♦ Although a higher percentage of claims is paid for orthopaedic wrong-site surgery than for other specialties, the dollar amounts paid are generally low. Furthermore, orthopaedic surgeons' wrong-site surgery claims are lower than the average amount paid for all orthopaedic claims.

♦ In most cases, the loss incurred was shared equally by the hospital and the physician.

♦ Knee arthroscopy and foot surgery procedures accounted for the most wrong-site surgeries.

♦ If the wrong site was discovered during the original anesthesia, the surgeon usually proceeded to the correct site and performed the correct procedure immediately.

♦ Most patients had no permanent disability from the wrong-site surgery.

♦ Wrong-site surgery can be prevented by having the surgeon operate through or adjacent to his or her initials placed preoperatively on the operative site.

♦ An intraoperative spinal x-ray should be obtained to confirm the appropriate level of spinal surgery.

Recommendations to the Board of Directors

♦ The Task Force on Wrong-site Surgery recommends that the American Academy of Orthopaedic Surgeons adopt the described method of prevention of wrong-site surgery and the advisory statement.

♦ An advisory statement should be formulated by the American Academy of Orthopaedic Surgeons to recommend this method of prevention and this information should be disseminated to the AAOS fellowship, resident training programs, and hospital personnel through CME courses, videotapes, and society newsletters and bulletins. Information about this method of prevention should be made available with an education campaign at AAOS Annual Meetings.

♦ AAOS Fellows and members, resident training programs, appropriate hospital and operating room personnel, and the national media should be informed of this method of prevention.

♦ Methods of dissemination of this educational material should include:

  ♦ Slide presentations or videotapes at AAOS CME courses

  ♦ Articles in the *AAOS Bulletin*, newsletters and other publications of state orthopaedic societies and specialty societies, and publications

♦ Scientific article for *Journal of the American Academy of Orthopaedic Surgeons* or editorial in the *Journal of Bone and Joint Surgery*

♦ Educational programs at annual meetings

♦ Exhibit (with handout) at annual meetings

♦ Information on the American Academy of Orthopaedic Surgeons home page on the Internet.

♦ The Committee on Professional Liability should investigate the possibility of malpractice premium reductions if this preventive program is carried out.

♦ Designated spokespersons to answer questions from the national media

Charges to the AAOS Task Force on Wrong-site Surgery

1. To determine the incidence of wrong-site surgery (wrong patient, extremity, digit, etc.) as it relates to orthopaedics.

2. To record the mechanisms that led to the wrong-site occurrence (eg, x-ray, chart, physician mistake).

3. To establish an acceptable protocol on how to proceed once discovery of the error has been made (stop or complete the correct surgery).

4. Summarize results of past litigation and possible legal relief for future.

5. Recommend to the Fellowship the method or methods to prevent and eliminate wrong-site surgery from occurring.

6. Determine the correct educational vehicles by which this information should be disseminated to the Fellowship (AV tape, symposium, etc.).

7. Decide whether this information should be disseminated to other medical and paramedical disciplines (eg, operating room directors, OR nurses, anesthesiologists, radiologists, radiology technicians).

American Academy of Orthopaedic Surgeons
Council on Education
January 1997

References

1. Physician Insurers Association of America (PIAA). Claims Data. Rockville, MD: PIAA, 1996

2. State Volunteer Mutual Insurance Company (SVMIC). Claims Data. Brentwood, TN: SVMIC, 1996

3. The Medical Defence Union, et al. *Theatre Safeguards*. London, 1988

4. The Canadian Orthopaedic Association Committee on Practice and Economics, *Position Paper on Wrong Sided Surgery in Orthopaedics.* Winnipeg, Manitoba: 10 Jun 1994

5. MAG Mutual Insurance Company. *Premium Reduction Program*, Atlanta, GA.

6. Paul H. Wright, MD. Letter to Jesse DeLee, MD. 9 Jul 96

7. Midwest Medical Insurance Company, Risk Management Advisory. Minneapolis, MN. MMIC, Feb 1997

PIAA Claim Data: Orthopaedic Surgery (1985–1998)

(References in this PIAA data section are to the accompanying data tables at the end of the section, Exhibits 1 through 10)

Executive Summary
Orthopaedic Surgery

This Executive Summary provides an overview of major areas of interest in the reports that follow. This summary, as well as the reports in their entirety, are not intended to be a formal position of the PIAA regarding the interpretation of the data found herein, but are intended to serve as an aid to those who wish to be informed of the data. The PIAA does not intend that the data contained herein be interpreted as defining standards of care attributable to the PIAA and makes no recommendation as to the use of data for such purposes. While every effort has been made to assure the compilation of reliable statistics, the PIAA does not guarantee or warrant the accuracy of this information.

These data have been reported in a codified manner. Reporting companies have been given explicit details as to the composition of the contents of the database and means by which to organize and code their own data. Definitions of fields such as the severity, medical misadventures and associated issues are provided for consistent use.

Procedures performed by practitioners and presenting patient conditions are coded using the International Classification of Diseases, Volume 9, Clinical Modification (ICD-9). Because of the great degree of detail in the ICD-9 coding scheme, the PIAA aggregates similar procedures and conditions to increase the usefulness of the reports. For example, when capturing data on displacement of intervertebral discs, all ICD-9 condition codes reported to the database between 722.00 and 722.90 are aggregated, without regard to location of the disc. However, the detailed code reported by member companies is retained in the database for reference if necessary.

Each section contains a brief analysis of the data contained herein. Please note that this executive summary is based on 1997 data; the exhibits include 1998 data, so numbers used in the summary do not match the exhibits exactly.

Insured Demographic Information (Exhibit 1)

The Data Sharing System captures demographic information on the insured physician. Information regarding the age, gender, board certification status, and previous claims experience are among the fields captured. The compiled data on orthopaedists are then compared to that of all physician specialties to observe deviations, if any, of the specialty group from the population of all specialties. Where possible, these data have also been compared to published AMA census data on this specialty group.

Age Group Data Orthopaedic surgeons with claims reported to the PIAA Data Sharing System are about the same age when

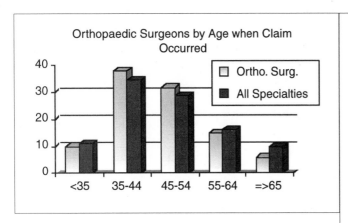

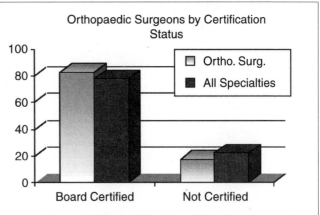

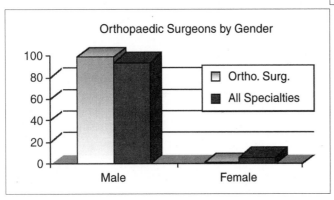

compared to all physician specialties. Just over 47% of orthopaedists were under 45 years old when the malpractice claim occurred. This compares to 45% for all physician specialties. At right is a graphic representation of orthopaedic surgeons by age compared to all specialty groups. The percentage of PIAA orthopaedists under age 45 is slightly less than those published by the AMA.[1] According to the AMA, 51% of orthopaedic surgeons are under the age of 45.

Gender Data   A very low percentage of female orthopaedists had claims than all physician specialties (0.8% vs. 5.7%). AMA statistics indicate that the overall percentage of female orthopaedic surgeons is as low as 2.7%.[2] Thus, fewer female orthopaedic surgeons have claims reported to the PIAA by percentage than are in practice.

Board Certification   Eighty-three percent of orthopaedic surgeons with claims reported

to the PIAA Data Sharing System are also board certified in that specialty, for those cases where board certification status was known. This compares to 77.8% of all board certified physicians with claims reported to the PIAA. The AMA figures show that 68.1% of all orthopaedists are board certified.[3]

Medical School   Eighty percent of orthopaedic surgeons with claims reported to the PIAA were graduates of U.S. medical schools. This is higher than the 71% for all physician specialties reported to the PIAA Data Sharing System. AMA figures show that 77.7% of all federal and nonfederal physicians are graduates of a medical school in the United States.

Previous Claims Experience   The number of orthopaedic surgeons with previous claims experience is considerably higher than that for all physician specialties (84% vs. 73%).

Payment Analysis by Specialty Group (Exhibit 2)

This report gives overall statistics regarding the number of claims reported and dollars paid for each specialty. Of the 28 specialty groups included in the database, orthopaedic surgery ranks 5th in the number of claims reported. The percentage of paid claims to those closed is 30.1%, or 1.7% less than that for all specialty groups.

The total indemnity paid on behalf of orthopaedic surgeons is $560.2 million, and also ranks 5th of the 28 specialty groups in monies paid. The cumulative average indemnity for this specialty group is 15.9% less than the overall average paid between 1985 and 1997 ($130,384 vs. $154,951).

Comparative Claim Payment Analysis (Exhibit 3)

A total of 237 paid orthopaedic surgery claims were reported to the PIAA in 1997. Total indemnity paid for these claims amounted to over $45.1 million. The average indemnity paid in 1997 was $190,694. The median payment was $91,375, which is below the median for all paid claims reported ($125,000). The largest payment reported in 1997 against this specialty group was $1.9 million, less than the largest payment reported ($2.7 million).

A comparable number of claims paid on behalf of general surgeons was reported to the database in 1997. General surgery claims resulted in an average payment about 12% higher than that of orthopaedic claims ($212,900 vs. $190,700). In addition, the median value of general surgery claims was 23% higher ($112,500 vs. $91,375).

Trend Analysis of Claims by Close Year (Exhibit 4)

In 1997, as previously mentioned, the average indemnity paid on behalf of orthopaedic surgeons was $190,694. This payment value is 20% less than the overall average indemnity paid for all physician specialties ($239,000). In 1992, the average indemnity payment for orthopaedic surgeons, $154,393,

was 16% less than the overall average of $183,580. In that five-year period, the average orthopaedic surgery indemnity has increased 23.5%. When adjusted for inflation, the increase in average payments between the two periods was 7.5%.

In 1997 orthopaedic surgery claims were a relatively significant percentage of claims reported to PIAA. Exactly 8.6% of claims and 7.2% of indemnity dollars were attributable to orthopaedic claims. These percentages have decreased slightly compared to a decade ago, when this specialty group made up 11.4% of claims and 8% of indemnity reported to PIAA.

Over 32.2% of orthopaedic surgery claims closed in 1997 resulted in an indemnity payment to the plaintiff. This percentage has gone up slightly from 28.1% a decade ago. This figure is comparable to the percentage for all physician specialty groups, in which 31% of all claims closed in 1997 resulted in a payment.

The amount of expenses spent to defend claims in 1997 was just above that for all specialty groups ($24,698 vs. $22,400). More than $18 million was reported in payments for the defense of 735 claims against this specialty group in 1997.

Claims by 10 Most Prevalent Medical Misadventures (Exhibit 5)

The first page of this exhibit lists the ten most prevalent medical misadventures reported against this specialty group. The most prevalent medical misadventure in orthopaedic surgery claims was improper performance, which was reported as the primary issue in 39% of claims reported between 1985 and 1997. For claims closed in 1997 only, improper performance was again the primary misadventure reported in 48% of claims. Moreover, 53% of claims paid in 1997 against this specialty group reported improper performance as the primary allegation.

For claims involving improper performance, operative procedures on joint structures (exclusive of spinal fusion) was the most prevalent condition improperly performed by this specialty group. Open reduction of dislocation, closed reduction of fractures, operative procedures on bones and skeletal traction followed this condition. Of these, improperly performed open reduction of dislocation resulted in the highest percentage of paid claims (41.5%) and improperly performed operative procedures on joint structures resulted in the highest average payment ($160,410).

Other prevalent medical misadventures reported were no medical misadventure, categorized as a situation where there is an absence of an allegation of any inappropriate medical conduct on the part of this insured. This was followed by diagnostic errors, procedures performed when not indicated or contraindicated and failure to supervise or monitor a case.

Claims by 10 Most Prevalent Patient Conditions (Exhibit 6)

The most common patient conditions for which claims were filed against orthopaedic surgeons were fracture of femur and fracture of tibia or fibula. Claims involving fracture of the femur resulted in an indemnity payment 32% of the time. The total indemnity paid for claims involving both fractures of the femur and tibia or fibula was 10% of the total paid for all orthopaedic surgery claims. For claims closed in 1997, the most prevalent patient conditions that resulted in claims

were fracture of the femur followed by disorders of joints (not including arthritis).

Claims by 10 Most Prevalent Procedures Performed (Exhibit 7)

Operative procedures on joint structures (exclusive of spinal fusion) were the procedures performed that resulted in the most claims against this physician specialty both in 1997 and in the cumulative data. Of the 14,258 orthopaedic surgery claims closed between 1985 and 1997, over 23% involved operative procedures on joint structures. Some $158.2 million of the $560.2 million (28%) paid on behalf of orthopaedic surgeons involved this procedure. The next most prevalent procedure resulting in claims against this specialty group was a diagnostic interview, evaluation, or consultation (12% of claims and 7.7% of indemnity).

Claims by Severity of the Patient's Injury (Exhibit 8)

In reviewing orthopaedic surgery claims by the severity of the injury, the patient expired in 6% of the claims reported between 1985 and 1997. The average payment when the alleged incident resulted in the patient's death was $163,682, approximately 28% higher than the cumulative average for all orthopaedic surgery claims that did not result in death.

The most prevalent severity was minor temporary injury, 25% of reported claims. For this group of claims, a payment resulted in 27.5% of the closed cases. However, more than 25% of the total indemnity paid on behalf of orthopaedic surgeons was for claims where the patient suffered minor permanent injury.

No medical misadventure was the most prevalent misadventure reported when the patient expired (24%). Not surprisingly, a payment was only made in 4.6% of these claims involving no medical misadventure. The patient condition most commonly reported in death cases was fracture of the femur. This condition combined with the second most prevalent, pulmonary embolism, made up 15% of all reported claims where the patient died. More than 24% of these closed claims resulted in indemnity payments totaling almost $6 million.

While representing only 1% of closed claims, when the treatment by an orthopaedic surgeon resulted in quadriplegia, brain damage, or need for lifelong care, the average payment was $386,194. The two most common conditions reported to result in this serious outcome are displacement of intervertebral disk and fracture of the vertebral column. These were also the only severities in which diagnostic errors were the most prevalent misadventure. In all other severities, no medical misadventure or improper performance were the most prevalent misadventures.

Claims that involve allegations of emotional trauma to the patient (and no physical injury) also represent just over 2% of closed claims against this specialty group. Only 12% of these claims resulted in an indemnity payment, with an average payment of $84,245. Not surprisingly, the most common medical misadventure reported was "no medical misadventure," which is commonly used in the absence of any evidence of medical negligence against the provider.

Claims by Associated Medical and Legal Issues (Exhibit 9)

For those cases in which an associated medicolegal issue was included in the allegation against the practitioner, consent issues, breach of contract, or warranty was second most prevalent behind the "other" category. More than 14% of the closed claims included consent issues as related in the case. Claims involving this issue resulted in an indemnity payment more than 41% of the time, and an average payment value of $127,363.

Claims by Associated Personnel (Exhibit 10)

This report identifies persons who had an association with the orthopaedic surgeon in the treatment that led to the allegations of negligence. Another physician, consultant of another specialty or the patient him/herself was identified as an associated person in the allegation in 24% of claims made against orthopaedic surgeons (3,771 of 15,729 claims). In 648 claims alone, it was felt that the patient's own actions somehow contributed to the allegations of negligence.

References

1. Physician Characteristics and Distribution in the U.S., 1994 Ed., Table B-5. American Medical Association, Chicago, IL. This edition was chosen because the majority of the claims reported to the PIAA occurred prior to 1995.

2. ibid. Table B-6, B-7.

3. ibid. Table B-12.

Insured Demographic Information
Orthopedic Surgery

Exhibit 1

Note: Number of physicians represented below differ because not all data fields are required. Further, some information is unknown and, therefore, not reflected in this report.

Cumulative Analysis: January 1, 1985 - December 31, 1998

AGE GROUPS	<35	35 - 44	45 - 54	55 - 64	>= 65	Total
	1,466	5,610	4,794	2,251	856	14,977

EMPLOYMENT STATUS

	Male	% of Total Male	Female	% of Total Female
Full Time	10,374	96.84	83	93.26
Part Time	339	3.16	6	6.74

GENDER

		% of Total
Male	10,713	99.18
Female	89	0.82

BOARD CERTIFIED

		% of Total
Yes	9,138	83.31
No	1,831	16.69

PREVIOUS CLAIMS EXPERIENCE

		% of Total
Yes	9,444	84.40
No	1,745	15.60

MEDICAL SCHOOL

		% of Total
U.S.	11,892	79.73
International	3,024	20.27

PRACTICE TYPE

		% of Total
Solo	6,709	44.80
Group	8,104	54.12
Institution	162	1.08

Exhibit 2

Comparative Claim Payment Analysis
Claims Closed Between 1985 and 1998

Cumulative Analysis: January 1, 1985 - December 31, 1998

Specialty Group	Closed Claims	Paid Claims	% Paid to Closed	Total Indemnity	Average Indemnity	Median Indemnity	Largest Payment
Anesthesiology	5,640	2,049	36.33	$366,195,796	$178,719	$45,000	$5,000,000
Cardiovascular Diseases - nonsurgical	2,004	391	19.51	$78,306,217	$200,272	$86,000	$1,850,000
Cardiovascular and Thoracic Surgery	4,021	969	24.10	$161,538,110	$166,706	$75,000	$2,050,000
Dentists	508	239	47.05	$8,068,372	$33,759	$13,500	$1,000,000
Dermatology - nonsurgical	1,627	518	31.84	$45,116,563	$87,098	$20,000	$1,350,000
Emergency Medicine - nonsurgical	2,082	599	28.77	$84,492,904	$141,057	$50,000	$1,625,000
Gastroenterology - nonsurgical	1,080	233	21.57	$30,000,223	$128,756	$65,000	$2,000,000
General Surgery	16,195	5,850	36.12	$856,453,215	$146,402	$66,667	$2,000,000
General and Family Practice - nonsurgical	17,034	6,323	37.12	$801,544,914	$126,767	$55,200	$2,500,000
Gynecology	1,726	572	33.14	$63,848,797	$111,624	$35,000	$2,900,000
Internal Medicine - nonsurgical	19,274	5,282	27.40	$846,741,532	$160,307	$75,000	$5,000,000
Neurology - nonsurgical	2,213	468	21.15	$111,831,051	$238,955	$100,000	$2,500,000
Neurosurgery	3,531	1,007	28.52	$243,024,321	$241,335	$100,000	$4,000,000
Obstetric and Gynecologic Surgery	20,725	7,558	36.47	$1,671,380,657	$221,141	$90,000	$2,024,568
Ophthalmology	4,322	1,310	30.31	$181,176,321	$138,303	$75,000	$2,024,568
Oral Surgery	47	17	36.17	$516,583	$30,387	$22,500	$133,500
Orthopedic Surgery	14,979	4,522	30.19	$603,418,371	$133,441	$60,000	$2,000,000
Other Nonsurgical Specialties	1,323	297	22.45	$35,097,406	$118,173	$30,000	$1,200,000
Otorhinolaryngology	2,378	775	32.59	$122,211,469	$157,692	$72,500	$4,000,000
Paraprofessional	189	43	22.75	$8,165,158	$189,887	$45,000	$1,322,290
Pathology - nonsurgical	1,002	305	30.44	$65,233,251	$213,880	$95,000	$2,000,000
Pediatrics - nonsurgical	4,558	1,344	29.49	$306,081,091	$227,739	$99,133	$4,418,041
Plastic Surgery	5,703	1,651	28.95	$142,645,675	$86,400	$31,250	$1,650,000
Psychiatry - nonsurgical	1,339	307	22.93	$32,885,667	$107,119	$42,500	$1,000,000
Radiation Therapy - nonsurgical	1,263	299	23.67	$62,434,861	$208,812	$75,000	$2,700,000
Radiology - nonsurgical	7,758	2,357	30.38	$316,507,917	$134,284	$54,000	$2,000,000
Resident/Intern	118	40	33.90	$2,335,932	$58,398	$47,500	$200,000
Urologic Surgery	3,648	1,117	30.62	$142,155,855	$127,266	$55,000	$2,904,241
TOTALS:	146,287	46,442	31.75	$7,389,408,229	$159,110	$65,000	$5,000,000

Exhibit 3

Comparative Claim Payment Analysis
Claims Closed in 1998

Specialty Group	Closed Claims	Paid Claims	% Paid to Closed	Total Indemnity	Average Indemnity	Median Indemnity	Largest Payment
Anesthesiology	247	66	26.72	$13,631,570	$206,539	$100,000	$1,200,000
Cardiovascular Diseases - nonsurgical	182	42	23.08	$12,935,448	$307,987	$195,000	$1,250,000
Cardiovascular and Thoracic Surgery	264	66	25.00	$12,695,285	$192,353	$100,000	$1,322,100
Dentists	97	35	36.08	$1,869,265	$53,408	$10,000	$1,000,000
Dermatology - nonsurgical	107	25	23.36	$3,784,751	$151,390	$77,500	$775,000
Emergency Medicine - nonsurgical	136	40	29.41	$6,902,500	$172,563	$81,875	$800,000
Gastroenterology - nonsurgical	62	9	14.52	$1,628,345	$180,927	$150,000	$400,000
General Surgery	867	312	35.99	$65,252,844	$209,144	$125,000	$2,000,000
General and Family Practice - nonsurgical	843	296	35.11	$63,676,927	$215,125	$113,500	$1,153,124
Gynecology	66	26	39.39	$3,462,171	$133,160	$77,500	$1,000,000
Internal Medicine - nonsurgical	1,135	324	28.55	$85,066,646	$262,551	$150,000	$2,900,000
Neurology - nonsurgical	103	21	20.39	$11,077,632	$527,506	$225,000	$5,000,000
Neurosurgery	177	45	25.42	$17,077,688	$379,504	$225,000	$1,000,000
Obstetric and Gynecologic Surgery	1,045	375	35.89	$126,454,671	$337,212	$200,000	$2,250,000
Ophthalmology	249	76	30.52	$17,132,504	$225,428	$135,000	$1,000,000
Oral Surgery	4	1	25.00	$12,500	$12,500	$12,500	$12,500
Orthopedic Surgery	635	200	31.50	$40,280,175	$201,401	$108,750	$2,000,000
Other Nonsurgical Specialties	99	22	22.22	$4,343,970	$197,453	$87,860	$900,000
Otorhinolaryngology	112	45	40.18	$12,051,087	$267,802	$90,000	$4,000,000
Paraprofessional	20	6	30.00	$1,126,000	$187,667	$88,000	$630,000
Pathology - nonsurgical	65	21	32.31	$6,978,000	$332,286	$300,000	$1,237,500
Pediatrics - nonsurgical	215	57	26.51	$15,553,407	$272,867	$190,000	$1,120,000
Plastic Surgery	268	73	27.24	$9,971,352	$136,594	$73,500	$1,000,000
Psychiatry - nonsurgical	70	20	28.57	$2,347,499	$117,375	$100,000	$287,500
Radiation Therapy - nonsurgical	152	46	30.26	$9,731,810	$211,561	$82,500	$1,800,000
Radiology - nonsurgical	461	158	34.27	$36,092,119	$228,431	$100,000	$1,000,000
Urologic Surgery	192	64	33.33	$14,162,601	$221,291	$90,000	$2,000,000
TOTALS:	7,873	2,471	31.39	$595,298,767	$240,914	$125,000	$5,000,000

Trend Analysis of Claims by Close Year
Orthopedic Surgery

Exhibit 4

	1988	1993	1998
Number of Closed Claims	1,353	1,195	635
Number of Paid Claims	377	368	200
% Paid to Closed Claims	27.86	30.79	31.50
Total Indemnity Paid	$43,091,566	$60,402,072	$40,280,175
Average Indemnity Paid	$114,301	$164,136	$201,401
Expenses Paid - All Claims	$15,477,967	$21,275,546	$15,972,753
Average Expense Paid	$11,440	$17,804	$25,154
Expenses Paid - Paid Claims	$6,440,193	$9,896,461	$6,604,322
Average Expenses Paid	$17,083	$26,893	$33,022
Expenses Paid - No Indemnity	$9,037,774	$11,379,085	$9,368,431
Average Expense Paid	$9,260	$13,759	$21,537

Comparative Claim Analysis
Orthopedic Surgery Claims to All Claims

	1988	1993	1998
Closed Claims - This Specialty	1,353	1,195	635
Closed Claims - All Specialties	11,954	12,366	7,873
% of All Closed Claims	11.32	9.66	8.07
Paid Claims - This Specialty	377	368	200
Paid Claims - All Specialties	3,845	3,796	2,471
% of All Paid Claims	9.80	9.69	8.09
Total Indemnity Paid - This Specialty	$43,091,566	$60,402,072	$40,280,175
Total Indemnity Paid - All Specialties	$487,393,082	$707,327,001	$595,298,767
% of All Indemnity Paid	8.84	8.54	6.77
Average Indemnity - This Specialty	$114,301	$164,136	$201,401
Average Indemnity - All Specialties	$126,760	$186,335	$240,914

Claims by 10 Most Prevalent Medical Misadventures
Orthopedic Surgery

Exhibit 5

Cumulative Analysis: January 1, 1985 - December 31, 1998

Medical Misadventure	Total Claims	Closed Claims	Paid Claims	% Paid to Closed	Total Indemnity	Average Indemnity
Improper performance	6,496	5,833	2,088	35.80	$285,942,275	$136,946
No medical misadventure	3,799	3,463	170	4.91	$19,631,301	$115,478
Errors in diagnosis	1,926	1,741	598	34.35	$83,706,165	$139,977
Performed when not indicated or contraindicated	823	774	264	34.11	$33,105,202	$125,398
Failure to supervise or monitor case	696	625	260	41.60	$42,291,728	$162,660
Failure to recognize a complication of treatment	581	515	228	44.27	$40,610,801	$178,118
Not performed	428	390	155	39.74	$19,575,312	$126,292
Wrong patient or body part	375	351	299	85.19	$17,616,042	$58,917
Delay in performance	275	258	107	41.47	$22,347,658	$208,857
Medication errors	256	240	88	36.67	$13,494,479	$153,346
TOTALS:	15,655	14,190	4,257	30.00	$578,320,963	$135,852

Closed in 1998 Only

Medical Misadventure	Closed Claims	Paid Claims	% Paid to Closed	Total Indemnity	Average Indemnity
Improper performance	300	105	35.00	$22,178,372	$211,223
No medical misadventure	101	8	7.92	$917,000	$114,625
Errors in diagnosis	58	21	36.21	$3,473,035	$165,383
Failure to supervise or monitor case	32	10	31.25	$4,736,822	$473,682
Failure to recognize a complication of treatment	27	8	29.63	$2,050,000	$256,250
Wrong patient or body part	21	17	80.95	$2,103,721	$123,721
Performed when not indicated or contraindicated	20	8	40.00	$2,165,001	$270,625
Not performed	14	4	28.57	$301,000	$75,250
Delay in performance	11	4	36.36	$527,500	$131,875
Surgical foreign body left in patient after proc	11	6	54.55	$246,120	$41,020
TOTALS:	595	191	32.10	$38,698,100	$202,608

Claims by Medical Misadventure and Procedure/Condition
Orthopedic Surgery

5 - 2

Cumulative Analysis: January 1, 1985 - December 31, 1998

Improper performance

Procedure	Total Claims	Closed Claims	Paid Claims	% Paid to Closed	Total Indemnity	Average Indemnity
Operative procedures on joint structures, exclusive of spinal fusion	2,028	1,812	636	35.10	$103,500,074	$162,736
Open reduction of dislocation, exclusive of facial bones	879	793	327	41.24	$44,742,215	$136,826
Closed reduction of fractures, exclusive of facial bones	737	675	247	36.59	$27,360,533	$110,771
Operative procedures on bones, exclusive of facial bones	588	528	214	40.53	$23,979,068	$112,052
Skeletal traction and other procedures involving immobilization	297	271	81	29.89	$7,707,773	$95,158
TOTALS:	4,529	4,079	1505	36.90	$207,289,663	$137,734

No medical misadventure

Condition	Total Claims	Closed Claims	Paid Claims	% Paid to Closed	Total Indemnity	Average Indemnity
Spondylosis & inflammatory spondylopathy	302	302	1	0.33	$49,500	$49,500
Femur, fracture of	164	152	7	4.61	$1,670,000	$238,571
Osteoarthrosis, generalized or localized	150	128	7	5.47	$2,220,000	$317,143
Fracture of the radius or ulna	142	127	5	3.94	$324,500	$64,900
Displacement of intervertebral disc	141	130	7	5.38	$1,003,078	$143,297
TOTALS:	899	839	27	3.22	$5,267,078	$195,077

Errors in diagnosis

Condition	Total Claims	Closed Claims	Paid Claims	% Paid to Closed	Total Indemnity	Average Indemnity
Foot, fracture of	81	77	24	31.17	$2,431,803	$101,325
Femur, fracture of	75	71	29	40.85	$2,870,133	$98,970
Fracture of the tibia or fibula	68	65	24	36.92	$4,797,699	$199,904
Fracture of vertebral column	65	59	22	37.29	$4,260,443	$193,657
Wrist bones, fracture of	53	49	24	48.98	$1,152,042	$48,002
TOTALS:	342	321	123	38.32	$15,512,120	$126,115

Claims by Medical Misadventure and Procedure/Condition
Orthopedic Surgery

5 - 3

Cumulative Analysis: January 1, 1985 - December 31, 1998

Performed when not indicated or contraindicated

Procedure	Total Claims	Closed Claims	Paid Claims	% Paid to Closed	Total Indemnity	Average Indemnity
Operative procedures on joint structures, exclusive of spinal fusion	190	178	56	31.46	$8,869,032	$158,376
Operative procedures on bones, exclusive of facial bones	96	87	42	48.28	$4,754,156	$113,194
Closed reduction of fractures, exclusive of facial bones	82	79	26	32.91	$2,047,429	$78,747
Open reduction of dislocation, exclusive of facial bones	79	73	24	32.88	$3,299,712	$137,488
Skeletal traction and other procedures involving immobilization	63	63	21	33.33	$3,219,995	$153,333
TOTALS:	510	480	169	35.21	$22,190,324	$131,304

Failure to supervise or monitor case

Condition	Total Claims	Closed Claims	Paid Claims	% Paid to Closed	Total Indemnity	Average Indemnity
Femur, fracture of	51	47	9	19.15	$816,312	$90,701
Osteoarthrosis, generalized or localized	26	21	5	23.81	$402,214	$80,443
Disorder of joint, not incl. arthritis	24	21	10	47.62	$1,762,802	$176,280
Fracture of the tibia or fibula	24	20	10	50.00	$2,326,449	$232,645
Fracture of the radius or ulna	20	17	6	35.29	$482,721	$80,454
TOTALS:	145	126	40	31.75	$5,790,498	$144,762

Exhibit 6

Claims by 10 Most Prevalent Patient Conditions
Orthopedic Surgery

Cumulative Analysis: January 1, 1985 - December 31, 1998

Patient Condition	Total Claims	Closed Claims	Paid Claims	% Paid to Closed	Total Indemnity	Average Indemnity
Femur, fracture of	879	820	261	31.83	$29,531,365	$113,147
Fracture of the tibia or fibula	760	689	204	29.61	$30,533,639	$149,675
Displacement of intervertebral disc	734	663	202	30.47	$46,086,474	$228,151
Osteoarthrosis, generalized or localized	699	627	196	31.26	$24,338,270	$124,175
Fracture of the radius or ulna	636	577	172	29.81	$12,618,199	$73,362
Disorder of joint, not incl. arthritis	556	469	128	27.29	$13,436,002	$104,969
Fracture of medial malleolus closed	466	415	147	35.42	$19,184,075	$130,504
Tear of medial cartilage or meniscus of knee	452	419	125	29.83	$14,581,003	$116,648
Back disorders, incl. lumbago & sciatica	426	379	90	23.75	$18,458,511	$205,095
Humerus, fracture of	357	307	97	31.60	$11,671,591	$120,326
TOTALS:	5,965	5,365	1,622	30.23	$220,439,129	$135,906

Closed in 1998 Only

Patient Condition	Closed Claims	Paid Claims	% Paid to Closed	Total Indemnity	Average Indemnity
Disorder of joint, not incl. arthritis	49	22	44.90	$3,551,128	$161,415
Osteoarthrosis, generalized or localized	37	9	24.32	$1,817,500	$201,944
Femur, fracture of	33	8	24.24	$1,736,750	$217,094
Fracture of medial malleolus closed	31	12	38.71	$4,232,500	$352,708
Fracture of the radius or ulna	30	9	30.00	$781,072	$86,786
Injury to multiple parts of body	28	8	28.57	$2,195,959	$274,495
Fracture of the tibia or fibula	27	6	22.22	$2,430,368	$405,061
Back disorders, incl. lumbago & sciatica	25	8	32.00	$3,405,845	$425,731
Displacement of intervertebral disc	23	8	34.78	$2,205,000	$275,625
Carpal tunnel syndrome	21	8	38.10	$678,000	$84,750
TOTALS:	304	98	32.24	$23,034,122	$235,042

Claims by 10 Most Prevalent Procedures Performed
Orthopedic Surgery

Exhibit 7

Cumulative Analysis: January 1, 1985 - December 31, 1998

Procedure Performed	Total Claims	Closed Claims	Paid Claims	% Paid to Closed	Total Indemnity	Average Indemnity
Operative procedures on joint structures, exclusive of spinal fusion	3,967	3,554	1,199	33.74	$171,515,424	$143,049
Diagnostic interview, evaluation, or consultation	1,930	1,761	321	18.23	$45,874,299	$142,911
Open reduction of dislocation, exclusive of facial bones	1,673	1,528	557	36.45	$83,564,952	$150,027
Closed reduction of fractures, exclusive of facial bones	1,590	1,475	495	33.56	$57,250,719	$115,658
Operative procedures on bones, exclusive of facial bones	1,158	1,055	382	36.21	$41,540,933	$108,746
Skeletal traction and other procedures involving immobilization	868	798	227	28.45	$26,369,521	$116,165
No care rendered	588	572	23	4.02	$808,583	$35,156
Spinal fusion	466	394	112	28.43	$28,726,862	$256,490
Operative procedures on spinal cord and spinal canal	424	380	129	33.95	$25,126,640	$194,780
Operative procedures on cranial and peripheral nerves	407	367	146	39.78	$18,813,597	$128,860
TOTALS:	13,071	11,884	3,591	30.22	$499,591,530	$139,123

Closed in 1998 Only

Procedure Performed		Closed Claims	Paid Claims	% Paid to Closed	Total Indemnity	Average Indemnity
Operative procedures on joint structures, exclusive of spinal fusion		182	69	37.91	$12,339,877	$178,839
Diagnostic interview, evaluation, or consultation		65	8	12.31	$2,912,495	$364,062
Open reduction of dislocation, exclusive of facial bones		57	21	36.84	$6,809,250	$324,250
Closed reduction of fractures, exclusive of facial bones		52	14	26.92	$2,468,368	$176,312
Operative procedures on bones, exclusive of facial bones		35	11	31.43	$1,652,500	$150,227
Skeletal traction and other procedures involving immobilization		32	5	15.63	$2,123,072	$424,614
Operative procedures on cranial and peripheral nerves		27	14	51.85	$2,067,673	$147,691
Spinal fusion		21	9	42.86	$2,505,886	$278,432
Operative procedures on muscle, tendon and fascia and bursa, except hand		19	6	31.58	$1,075,000	$179,167
Diagnostic radiologic procedures, excluding CAT scan and contrast material		17	10	58.82	$1,102,500	$110,250
TOTALS:		507	167	32.94	$35,056,621	$209,920

Exhibit 8

Claims by Severity of the Patient's Injury
Orthopedic Surgery

Cumulative Analysis: January 1, 1985 - December 31, 1998

Severity of Injury	Total Claims	Closed Claims	Paid Claims	% Paid to Closed	Total Indemnity	Average Indemnity
Emotional injury only	362	341	41	12.02	$3,379,787	$82,434
Insignificant injury	815	776	162	20.88	$4,725,710	$29,171
Minor temporary injury	4,116	3,807	1,049	27.55	$72,302,374	$68,925
Major temporary injury	3,583	3,261	928	28.46	$105,817,555	$114,028
Minor permanent injury	3,822	3,455	1,184	34.27	$156,832,674	$132,460
Significant permanent injury	2,045	1,807	674	37.30	$141,072,126	$209,306
Major permanent injury	547	475	201	42.32	$63,836,564	$317,595
Quadriplegic, brain damage, lifelong care	176	151	41	27.15	$15,742,772	$383,970
Death	1,038	906	242	26.71	$39,708,809	$164,086
TOTALS:	16,504	14,979	4,522	30.19	$603,418,371	$133,441

Closed in 1998 Only

Severity of Injury		Closed Claims	Paid Claims	% Paid to Closed	Total Indemnity	Average Indemnity
Emotional injury only		9	0	0.00	$0	$0
Insignificant injury		21	3	14.29	$78,100	$26,033
Minor temporary injury		133	38	28.57	$2,842,661	$74,807
Major temporary injury		124	42	33.87	$8,446,824	$201,115
Minor permanent injury		200	70	35.00	$13,603,179	$194,331
Significant permanent injury		84	27	32.14	$7,671,911	$284,145
Major permanent injury		39	15	38.46	$6,567,500	$437,833
Quadriplegic, brain damage, lifelong care		5	1	20.00	$295,000	$295,000
Death		20	4	20.00	$775,000	$193,750
TOTALS:		635	200	31.50	$40,280,175	$201,401

Misadventure and Condition Analysis by Severity Index
Orthopedic Surgery

Cumulative Analysis: January 1, 1985 - December 31, 1998

Emotional injury only

Medical Misadventure	Total Claims	Closed Claims	Paid Claims	% Paid to Closed	Total Indemnity	Average Indemnity
No medical misadventure	191	182	11	6.04	$376,700	$34,245
Improper performance	63	59	8	13.56	$1,617,500	$202,188
Errors in diagnosis	17	14	1	7.14	$9,999	$9,999
Failure to instruct or communicate with patient	17	16	5	31.25	$47,499	$9,500
Performed when not indicated or contraindicated	15	14	5	35.71	$552,106	$110,421
Improper supervision of residents/other staff	13	13	0	0.00	$0	$0
Not performed	7	7	1	14.29	$10,000	$10,000
Wrong patient or body part	7	5	5	100.00	$133,483	$26,697
Delay in performance	6	5	3	60.00	$603,500	$201,167
Failure to supervise or monitor case	6	6	2	33.33	$29,000	$14,500
TOTALS:	342	321	41	12.77	$3,379,787	$82,434

Patient Condition	Total Claims	Closed Claims	Paid Claims	% Paid to Closed	Total Indemnity	Average Indemnity
Back disorders, incl. lumbago & sciatica	18	18	0	0.00	$0	$0
Femur, fracture of	16	15	2	13.33	$102,500	$51,250
Displacement of intervertebral disc	15	15	2	13.33	$95,000	$47,500
Disorder of joint, not incl. arthritis	12	11	0	0.00	$0	$0
Enthesopathies and other rheumatic disorders, excl. back	12	11	0	0.00	$0	$0
Hip, fracture of	10	10	0	0.00	$0	$0
Internal derangement of knee, incl. medial meniscus	10	10	1	10.00	$5,000	$5,000
Osteoarthrosis, generalized or localized	10	9	0	0.00	$0	$0
Tear of medial cartilage or meniscus of knee	10	10	1	10.00	$9,950	$9,950
Fracture of medial malleolus closed	9	9	4	44.44	$23,000	$5,750
TOTALS:	122	118	10	8.47	$235,450	$23,545

8 - 3

Misadventure and Condition Analysis by Severity Index
Orthopedic Surgery

Cumulative Analysis: January 1, 1985 - December 31, 1998

Insignificant injury

Medical Misadventure	Total Claims	Closed Claims	Paid Claims	% Paid to Closed	Total Indemnity	Average Indemnity
No medical misadventure	419	398	20	5.03	$1,040,199	$52,010
Improper performance	199	188	57	30.32	$1,444,807	$25,347
Wrong patient or body part	57	56	45	80.36	$836,840	$18,596
Errors in diagnosis	28	27	5	18.52	$126,100	$25,220
Surgical foreign body left in patient after proc	24	23	8	34.78	$117,375	$14,672
Failure to supervise or monitor case	18	18	7	38.89	$702,739	$100,391
Performed when not indicated or contraindicated	17	16	1	6.25	$175,000	$175,000
Medication errors	14	13	6	46.15	$122,500	$20,417
Failure to recognize a complication of treatment	9	8	4	50.00	$11,964	$2,991
Not performed	8	7	2	28.57	$61,750	$30,875
TOTALS:	**793**	**754**	**155**	**20.56**	**$4,639,274**	**$29,931**

Patient Condition	Total Claims	Closed Claims	Paid Claims	% Paid to Closed	Total Indemnity	Average Indemnity
Disorder of joint, not incl. arthritis	42	38	3	7.89	$44,000	$14,667
Back disorders, incl. lumbago & sciatica	37	35	2	5.71	$1,110,239	$555,120
Osteoarthrosis, generalized or localized	34	31	6	19.35	$120,000	$20,000
Internal derangement of knee, incl. medial meniscus	29	29	9	31.03	$209,000	$23,222
Tear of medial cartilage or meniscus of knee	28	24	9	37.50	$90,750	$10,083
Fracture of the radius or ulna	26	23	7	30.43	$114,879	$16,411
Fracture of the tibia or fibula	26	26	3	11.54	$42,900	$14,300
Displacement of intervertebral disc	22	21	2	9.52	$22,500	$11,250
Foot, fracture of	22	21	5	23.81	$123,600	$24,720
Enthesopathies and other rheumatic disorders, excl. back	19	17	4	23.53	$34,874	$8,719
TOTALS:	**285**	**265**	**50**	**18.87**	**$1,912,742**	**$38,255**

Misadventure and Condition Analysis by Severity Index
Orthopedic Surgery

Cumulative Analysis: January 1, 1985 - December 31, 1998

Minor temporary injury

Medical Misadventure	Total Claims	Closed Claims	Paid Claims	% Paid to Closed	Total Indemnity	Average Indemnity
Improper performance	1,635	1,512	462	30.56	$34,763,126	$75,245
No medical misadventure	949	845	53	6.27	$3,703,901	$69,885
Errors in diagnosis	452	422	126	29.86	$9,093,529	$72,171
Failure to supervise or monitor case	213	201	64	31.84	$6,068,140	$94,815
Performed when not indicated or contraindicated	175	166	49	29.52	$2,497,479	$50,969
Wrong patient or body part	126	121	110	90.91	$3,783,846	$34,399
Not performed	117	111	43	38.74	$3,903,461	$90,778
Failure to recognize a complication of treatment	108	103	34	33.01	$2,746,963	$80,793
Surgical foreign body left in patient after proc	87	82	37	45.12	$751,369	$20,307
Failure to instruct or communicate with patient	61	60	13	21.67	$425,001	$32,692
TOTALS:	3,923	3,623	991	27.35	$67,736,815	$68,352

Patient Condition	Total Claims	Closed Claims	Paid Claims	% Paid to Closed	Total Indemnity	Average Indemnity
Femur, fracture of	219	209	55	26.32	$3,814,558	$69,356
Fracture of the radius or ulna	215	194	52	26.80	$2,022,829	$38,901
Fracture of the tibia or fibula	212	198	45	22.73	$3,123,035	$69,401
Disorder of joint, not incl. arthritis	160	150	38	25.33	$3,121,931	$82,156
Tear of medial cartilage or meniscus of knee	153	148	45	30.41	$2,230,746	$49,572
Fracture of medial malleolus closed	151	131	42	32.06	$3,335,849	$79,425
Foot, fracture of	112	108	24	22.22	$1,225,603	$51,067
Wrist bones, fracture of	110	103	31	30.10	$1,689,960	$54,515
Humerus, fracture of	109	91	21	23.08	$1,839,299	$87,586
Osteoarthrosis, generalized or localized	106	96	28	29.17	$2,520,004	$90,000
TOTALS:	1,547	1,428	381	26.68	$24,923,814	$65,417

8 - 5

Misadventure and Condition Analysis by Severity Index
Orthopedic Surgery

Cumulative Analysis: January 1, 1985 - December 31, 1998

Major temporary injury

Medical Misadventure	Total Claims	Closed Claims	Paid Claims	% Paid to Closed	Total Indemnity	Average Indemnity
Improper performance	1,408	1,257	446	35.48	$52,755,084	$118,285
No medical misadventure	885	794	21	2.64	$2,137,582	$101,790
Errors in diagnosis	382	364	109	29.95	$11,111,206	$101,938
Performed when not indicated or contraindicated	193	188	65	34.57	$7,134,100	$109,755
Failure to recognize a complication of treatment	135	122	57	46.72	$7,925,050	$139,036
Failure to supervise or monitor case	120	105	45	42.86	$8,066,313	$179,251
Not performed	99	91	32	35.16	$3,861,069	$120,658
Surgical foreign body left in patient after proc	72	70	36	51.43	$2,189,059	$60,807
Delay in performance	70	67	19	28.36	$3,193,000	$168,053
Wrong patient or body part	63	57	50	87.72	$4,098,797	$81,976
TOTALS:	3,427	3,115	880	28.25	$102,471,260	$116,445

Patient Condition	Total Claims	Closed Claims	Paid Claims	% Paid to Closed	Total Indemnity	Average Indemnity
Spondylosis & inflammatory spondylopathy	303	301	2	0.66	$80,000	$40,000
Femur, fracture of	196	190	69	36.32	$6,670,245	$96,670
Displacement of intervertebral disc	192	174	39	22.41	$7,454,837	$191,150
Osteoarthrosis, generalized or localized	179	159	50	31.45	$5,444,473	$108,889
Fracture of the radius or ulna	132	121	38	31.40	$2,429,099	$63,924
Fracture of the tibia or fibula	128	113	31	27.43	$5,023,618	$162,052
Fracture of medial malleolus closed	102	95	38	40.00	$3,052,300	$80,324
Tear of medial cartilage or meniscus of knee	102	96	28	29.17	$2,862,896	$102,246
Back disorders, incl. lumbago & sciatica	96	84	22	26.19	$3,069,413	$139,519
Internal derangement of knee, incl. medial meniscus	88	80	23	28.75	$2,866,275	$124,621
TOTALS:	1,518	1,413	340	24.06	$38,953,156	$114,568

Misadventure and Condition Analysis by Severity Index
Orthopedic Surgery

Cumulative Analysis: January 1, 1985 - December 31, 1998

Minor permanent injury

Medical Misadventure	Total Claims	Closed Claims	Paid Claims	% Paid to Closed	Total Indemnity	Average Indemnity
Improper performance	1,805	1,598	618	38.67	$80,613,535	$130,443
No medical misadventure	721	671	35	5.22	$6,348,167	$181,376
Errors in diagnosis	357	318	131	41.19	$18,159,934	$138,625
Performed when not indicated or contraindicated	211	198	66	33.33	$8,990,558	$136,221
Failure to recognize a complication of treatment	137	123	64	52.03	$10,422,914	$162,858
Failure to supervise or monitor case	129	116	54	46.55	$8,876,548	$164,381
Not performed	101	92	42	45.65	$4,127,202	$98,267
Wrong patient or body part	90	85	72	84.71	$5,414,083	$75,196
Failure to instruct or communicate with patient	62	55	15	27.27	$750,343	$50,023
Delay in performance	58	55	30	54.55	$4,046,750	$134,892
TOTALS:	3,671	3,311	1,127	34.04	$147,750,034	$131,100

Patient Condition	Total Claims	Closed Claims	Paid Claims	% Paid to Closed	Total Indemnity	Average Indemnity
Osteoarthrosis, generalized or localized	218	202	68	33.66	$8,529,695	$125,437
Femur, fracture of	212	197	74	37.56	$9,545,402	$128,992
Fracture of the radius or ulna	199	185	59	31.89	$5,248,729	$88,962
Fracture of the tibia or fibula	196	178	63	35.39	$9,154,390	$145,308
Displacement of intervertebral disc	162	143	49	34.27	$9,954,120	$203,145
Disorder of joint, not incl. arthritis	160	127	39	30.71	$4,162,692	$106,736
Tear of medial cartilage or meniscus of knee	97	85	24	28.24	$2,199,912	$91,663
Carpal tunnel syndrome	91	84	39	46.43	$4,713,729	$120,865
Fracture of medial malleolus closed	91	83	28	33.73	$4,845,074	$173,038
Foot, fracture of	89	80	32	40.00	$3,065,400	$95,794
TOTALS:	1,515	1,364	475	34.82	$61,419,143	$129,303

Misadventure and Condition Analysis by Severity Index
Orthopedic Surgery

8 - 7

Cumulative Analysis: January 1, 1985 - December 31, 1998

Significant permanent injury

Medical Misadventure	Total Claims	Closed Claims	Paid Claims	% Paid to Closed	Total Indemnity	Average Indemnity
Improper performance	971	861	363	42.16	$77,315,251	$212,990
Errors in diagnosis	283	236	85	36.02	$18,416,402	$216,664
No medical misadventure	268	243	11	4.53	$1,703,002	$154,818
Performed when not indicated or contraindicated	117	106	48	45.28	$7,079,373	$147,487
Failure to supervise or monitor case	85	73	40	54.79	$8,288,286	$207,207
Failure to recognize a complication of treatment	82	72	34	47.22	$8,832,299	$259,774
Delay in performance	51	49	28	57.14	$7,903,914	$282,283
Not performed	50	46	18	39.13	$3,574,189	$198,566
Medication errors	27	26	8	30.77	$1,561,999	$195,250
Wrong patient or body part	27	23	14	60.87	$3,053,993	$218,142
TOTALS:	1,961	1,735	649	37.41	$137,728,708	$212,217

Patient Condition	Total Claims	Closed Claims	Paid Claims	% Paid to Closed	Total Indemnity	Average Indemnity
Displacement of intervertebral disc	168	151	56	37.09	$15,433,485	$275,598
Fracture of the tibia or fibula	145	129	45	34.88	$8,811,653	$195,815
Femur, fracture of	115	102	35	34.31	$5,388,203	$153,949
Osteoarthrosis, generalized or localized	96	82	28	34.15	$2,817,364	$100,620
Fracture of medial malleolus closed	58	50	23	46.00	$3,686,175	$160,268
Disorder of joint, not incl. arthritis	47	39	17	43.59	$2,629,417	$154,672
Foot, fracture of	44	38	9	23.68	$1,626,188	$180,688
Back disorders, incl. lumbago & sciatica	43	40	11	27.50	$3,429,379	$311,762
Humerus, fracture of	43	40	24	60.00	$3,736,823	$155,701
Fracture of the radius or ulna	41	36	14	38.89	$2,792,663	$199,476
TOTALS:	800	707	262	37.06	$50,351,350	$192,181

Misadventure and Condition Analysis by Severity Index
Orthopedic Surgery

Cumulative Analysis: January 1, 1985 - December 31, 1998

Major permanent injury

Medical Misadventure	Total Claims	Closed Claims	Paid Claims	% Paid to Closed	Total Indemnity	Average Indemnity
Improper performance	188	159	75	47.17	$24,900,710	$332,009
Errors in diagnosis	105	96	40	41.67	$10,047,137	$251,178
No medical misadventure	92	81	8	9.88	$2,838,750	$354,844
Failure to recognize a complication of treatment	45	36	25	69.44	$7,373,227	$294,929
Performed when not indicated or contraindicated	28	28	14	50.00	$4,113,879	$293,849
Failure to supervise or monitor case	22	17	13	76.47	$3,831,708	$294,747
Not performed	12	10	5	50.00	$2,053,641	$410,728
Delay in performance	11	9	5	55.56	$2,372,000	$474,400
Failure to instruct or communicate with patient	9	7	2	28.57	$762,500	$381,250
Medication errors	9	9	2	22.22	$1,330,012	$665,006
TOTALS:	521	452	189	41.81	$59,623,564	$315,469

Patient Condition	Total Claims	Closed Claims	Paid Claims	% Paid to Closed	Total Indemnity	Average Indemnity
Displacement of intervertebral disc	45	44	21	47.73	$8,443,417	$402,067
Back disorders, incl. lumbago & sciatica	33	31	18	58.06	$4,924,677	$273,593
Fracture of vertebral column	32	29	13	44.83	$3,541,168	$272,398
Femur, fracture of	21	19	7	36.84	$1,642,500	$234,643
Stenosis, spinal, other than cervical	20	17	11	64.71	$2,112,284	$192,026
Disorder of joint, not incl. arthritis	16	11	3	27.27	$464,000	$154,667
Injury to multiple parts of body	15	10	4	40.00	$1,380,000	$345,000
Fracture of medial malleolus closed	14	12	4	33.33	$2,582,177	$645,544
Osteoarthrosis, generalized or localized	13	12	9	75.00	$3,056,734	$339,637
Fracture of the tibia or fibula	12	11	8	72.73	$3,132,210	$391,526
TOTALS:	221	196	98	50.00	$31,279,167	$319,175

Misadventure and Condition Analysis by Severity Index
Orthopedic Surgery

8 - 9

Cumulative Analysis: January 1, 1985 - December 31, 1998

Quadriplegic, brain damage, lifelong care

Medical Misadventure	Total Claims	Closed Claims	Paid Claims	% Paid to Closed	Total Indemnity	Average Indemnity
Errors in diagnosis	67	55	23	41.82	$7,083,927	$307,997
Improper performance	37	32	8	25.00	$3,325,846	$415,731
No medical misadventure	32	31	1	3.23	$300,000	$300,000
Failure to supervise or monitor case	10	10	4	40.00	$2,629,999	$657,500
Performed when not indicated or contraindicated	8	5	2	40.00	$1,003,000	$501,500
Failure to recognize a complication of treatment	5	5	1	20.00	$500,000	$500,000
Medication errors	4	3	0	0.00	$0	$0
Delay in performance	3	3	2	66.67	$900,000	$450,000
Failure to instruct or communicate with patient	2	1	0	0.00	$0	$0
Not performed	2	2	0	0.00	$0	$0
TOTALS:	**170**	**147**	**41**	**27.89**	**$15,742,772**	**$383,970**

Patient Condition	Total Claims	Closed Claims	Paid Claims	% Paid to Closed	Total Indemnity	Average Indemnity
Displacement of intervertebral disc	12	9	5	55.56	$1,566,262	$313,252
Fracture of vertebral column	12	10	4	40.00	$2,370,000	$592,500
Back disorders, incl. lumbago & sciatica	8	6	1	16.67	$100,000	$100,000
Malignant neoplasms of the bronchus and lung	8	8	1	12.50	$75,000	$75,000
Disorders of soft tissue	5	4	0	0.00	$0	$0
Malignant neoplasms of the bones of upper limb	5	5	3	60.00	$317,553	$105,851
Multiple myeloma	4	4	2	50.00	$400,000	$200,000
Osteoarthrosis, generalized or localized	4	2	0	0.00	$0	$0
Spondylosis & inflammatory spondylopathy	4	4	3	75.00	$1,521,954	$507,318
Congenital anomalies of spine	3	3	0	0.00	$0	$0
TOTALS:	**65**	**55**	**19**	**34.55**	**$6,350,769**	**$334,251**

8 - 10

Misadventure and Condition Analysis by Severity Index
Orthopedic Surgery

Cumulative Analysis: January 1, 1985 - December 31, 1998

Death

Medical Misadventure	Total Claims	Closed Claims	Paid Claims	% Paid to Closed	Total Indemnity	Average Indemnity
No medical misadventure	242	218	10	4.59	$1,183,000	$118,300
Errors in diagnosis	235	209	78	37.32	$9,657,931	$123,820
Improper performance	190	167	51	30.54	$9,206,416	$180,518
Failure to supervise or monitor case	93	79	31	39.24	$3,798,995	$122,548
Performed when not indicated or contraindicated	59	53	14	26.42	$1,559,707	$111,408
Medication errors	57	49	17	34.69	$4,616,332	$271,549
Failure to recognize a complication of treatment	56	42	9	21.43	$2,798,384	$310,932
Not performed	32	24	12	50.00	$1,984,000	$165,333
Improper supervision of residents/other staff	19	19	1	5.26	$600,000	$600,000
Failure/delay in referral or consultation	18	15	6	40.00	$1,610,000	$268,333
TOTALS:	1,001	875	229	26.17	$37,014,765	$161,637

Patient Condition	Total Claims	Closed Claims	Paid Claims	% Paid to Closed	Total Indemnity	Average Indemnity
Femur, fracture of	90	78	17	21.79	$2,352,957	$138,409
Pulmonary embolism	64	56	16	28.57	$3,642,892	$227,681
Osteoarthrosis, generalized or localized	39	34	7	20.59	$1,850,000	$264,286
Malignant neoplasms of the bronchus and lung	37	36	10	27.78	$1,948,361	$194,836
Fracture of the tibia or fibula	35	28	9	32.14	$1,245,833	$138,426
Disorder of joint, not incl. arthritis	33	26	8	30.77	$547,223	$68,403
Fracture of medial malleolus closed	30	24	6	25.00	$1,157,500	$192,917
Back disorders, incl. lumbago & sciatica	25	20	4	20.00	$964,999	$241,250
Hip, fracture of	24	21	3	14.29	$214,999	$71,666
Displacement of intervertebral disc	20	18	5	27.78	$1,643,000	$328,600
TOTALS:	397	341	85	24.93	$15,567,764	$183,150

Claims by Associated Medical and Legal Issues
Orthopedic Surgery

Exhibit 9

Cumulative Analysis: January 1, 1985 - December 31, 1998

Associated Issue	Total Claims	Closed Claims	Paid Claims	% Paid to Closed	Total Indemnity	Average Indemnity
Other	4,940	4,277	836	19.55	$114,492,856	$136,953
Consent Issues, Breach of Contract or Warranty	1,497	1,363	444	32.58	$62,073,890	$139,806
Surgical/Medical Device	399	382	14	3.66	$2,128,750	$152,054
Vicarious Liability	321	304	86	28.29	$11,863,244	$137,945
Equipment Malfunction or Utilization Problem	296	271	102	37.64	$12,028,997	$117,931
Problems with Records	237	227	124	54.63	$18,932,490	$152,681
X-ray Error	222	201	106	52.74	$12,342,637	$116,440
Billing and Collection	191	188	33	17.55	$2,247,750	$68,114
Punitive Damages	182	172	65	37.79	$10,306,254	$158,558
Premature Discharge from Institution	147	137	78	56.93	$14,574,930	$186,858
Lack of Adequate Facilities or Equipment	144	134	66	49.25	$9,465,763	$143,421
Abandonment	109	98	33	33.67	$5,684,585	$172,260
Assault and Battery	91	83	43	51.81	$6,262,598	$145,642
Improper Conduct by Physician	88	77	33	42.86	$4,143,566	$125,563
Communication Between Providers	68	53	16	30.19	$2,393,524	$149,595
Failure to Conform with Regulation/Statute/Rule	49	45	12	26.67	$1,145,472	$95,456
Unnecessary Treatment	46	39	15	38.46	$1,707,200	$113,813
Res ipsa loquitur - self evident	31	26	17	65.38	$2,257,958	$132,821
Breach of Confidentiality	28	26	5	19.23	$250,927	$50,185
Laboratory Error	23	22	9	40.91	$2,161,000	$240,111
Pharmacy Error	15	14	5	35.71	$553,500	$110,700
Aseptic Technique	11	8	3	37.50	$400,000	$133,333
Third Party Claimant	8	8	1	12.50	$95,000	$95,000
False Imprisonment	5	4	1	25.00	$27,499	$27,499
Managed Care Referral Problem	4	3	0	0.00	$0	$0
Religious Issues	1	1	0	0.00	$0	$0
TOTALS:	9,153	8,163	2,147	26.30	$297,540,390	$138,584

Claims by Associated Personnel
Orthopedic Surgery

Exhibit 10

Cumulative Analysis: January 1, 1985 - December 31, 1998

Associated Personnel	Total Claims	Closed Claims	Paid Claims	% Paid to Closed	Total Indemnity	Average Indemnity
Other Physician	4,374	3,804	1,075	28.26	$185,527,382	$172,584
Patient	921	865	175	20.23	$22,084,215	$126,196
Consultant	857	783	298	38.06	$62,391,507	$209,367
Radiologist	657	597	234	39.20	$34,692,641	$148,259
Other Person or Personnel	638	594	106	17.85	$17,001,221	$160,389
Nurse	580	539	260	48.24	$28,119,773	$108,153
Resident or Intern	525	498	207	41.57	$39,599,284	$191,301
Emergency Medicine Physician	524	499	174	34.87	$21,821,165	$125,409
Anesthesiologist	294	253	77	30.43	$12,313,251	$159,912
Physical Therapist	256	231	70	30.30	$13,816,575	$197,380
Other Hospital Personnel	228	204	81	39.71	$6,658,785	$82,207
Technician	146	135	66	48.89	$5,575,865	$84,483
Physician's Assistant	77	73	34	46.58	$2,460,265	$72,361
Pathologist	59	56	26	46.43	$4,931,582	$189,676
Dentist	58	55	18	32.73	$3,369,528	$187,196
Chiropractor	56	53	13	24.53	$2,237,545	$172,119
Nurse Anesthetist	53	49	17	34.69	$2,276,764	$133,927
Podiatrist	52	45	7	15.56	$505,789	$72,256
Family Members	17	14	4	28.57	$71,000	$17,750
Pharmacist	10	9	3	33.33	$144,850	$48,283
Nurse Practitioner	8	8	2	25.00	$209,000	$104,500
Other Therapist	8	7	4	57.14	$580,000	$145,000
Other Office Personnel	7	7	3	42.86	$181,500	$60,500
Nurse Midwife	3	2	1	50.00	$100,000	$100,000
TOTALS:	10,408	9,380	2,955	31.50	$466,669,487	$157,925

Glossary of Terms

Professional Liability Coverage The policy covers professional services rendered from which an act or omission must arise for coverage to be applicable. Coverage typically includes all services rendered in the insured's professional capacity, and excludes dishonest, fraudulent, or criminal acts or omissions, as well as general exclusions for bodily injury, property damages, etc. Policies vary from company to company with respect to coverage for activities such as peer review, committee service, etc.

Types of Policy Coverage

Claims Made Coverage A policy that covers an insured against claims reported during the policy period regardless of when the event occurred.

Group Coverage Coverage extended to multiple physicians by one policy, applicable to incidents reported on behalf of all physicians named on the declarations page of the policy.

Individual Coverage The policy specifies that coverage is provided to one physician, with one policy limit, applicable only to acts or omissions of that physician.

Locum Tenens Coverage Coverage provided to an additional physician who is temporarily replacing the policyholder in his/her medical practice.

Nose Coverage This coverage provides coverage for claims that arise from prior wrongful acts or omissions of the insured that took place before the retroactive date. The retroactive date is the date on which the policy is first in effect. The retroactive date of the policy is extended backward in time to provide coverage for a specified period, and will thereby obviate the need for purchase of "tail coverage" from the prior insurer.

Occurrence Coverage A policy type that covers an insured against claims that arise from an event during the policy period, regardless of when the claim is reported.

Partnership/Corporation Coverage Provides coverage against the liability of an insured arising out of the partnership or corporation of which the physician is an owner or shareholder.

Slot Coverage A type of coverage offered typically to group practices or institutions, covering the risks of a "block" of exposures such as the several physicians rotating through a full-time equivalent position. In a large group practice there may be more than one physician rotating in and out of the "slot" and the coverage applies to each during his/her time in the practice.

Tail Coverage Also know as an extended reporting endorsement. This policy or endorsement type provides coverage for claims caused by errors or omissions occurring during a policy period but not reported until after a policy expires or has been canceled.

Vicarious Liability   Liability imposed upon a physician for the acts or omissions of others. Professional liability policies generally cover this exposure for the acts of other health professionals working under the supervision of the insured physician.

Coverages

Basic/Primary Coverage   Primary insurance provides coverage for liability which attaches immediately upon the filing of a claim.

Deductible Policy   A professional liability policy that requires a specified, per claim payment by the insured. The deductible amount may apply only to damages paid to claimants, or may include loss adjusting expenses of the company.

Excess Coverage   Available only if the insured maintains primary coverage, this provides coverage only after the predetermined limits of primary insurance have been exhausted.

Patient Compensation/Catastrophic Coverage   Several states have catastrophic or patient compensation funds which provide an additional layer of coverage beyond the physician's primary insurance policy limits.

Reinsurance   Purchased by insurers to provide coverage for losses above a specified dollar limit.

Policy Terms

Accident/Incident Date   The date on which the alleged injury occurred, also referred to as the occurrence date.

Aggregate Limits   The amount of coverage provided by the policy for the total of all indemnity payments to plaintiffs paid during the policy period.

Alternative Dispute Resolution (ADR) Various voluntary or contractual methods of claim resolution employed in an attempt to achieve more expeditious resolution of claims. These include arbitration, mediation, settlement conferences, and other specialized techniques, and may in some instances serve to reduce the time and expense involved in claim resolution.

Bad Faith   A legal concept, applicable to the actions of an insurance company, which may protect the interests of a policyholder in certain instances. Should a company lose a judgment in excess of the insured's policy limits, rather than having honored the pretrial demand of insured or counsel that a claim be settled within those limits, the court may, in a subsequent action, award damages to the insured based upon the "bad faith" actions of the company.

Basic Limits   The amount of coverage provided by the policy for indemnity payments to plaintiffs for each claim paid during the policy period.

Claim   Any demand for compensation, with no legal papers actually filed in court. Policy provisions require that any such demand must be immediately reported to the insurance company.

Consent to Settle   A policy provision which mandates that the company may not settle on the insured's behalf without first obtaining written consent of the insured.

Coverage Damages   Indemnity losses paid to plaintiffs, these traditionally include economic losses and noneconomic damages associated with the payment (pain and suffering, loss of consortium, etc.). Nearly all insurance policies do not cover punitive damages, and that fact will be noted in the policy language.

Declarations Page   The page on the issued insurance policy that states in detail specifics of the policy provisions regarding practice type and location, specialty, endorsed procedures if applicable, etc. This page contains the information on which the insurance premium is computed.

Defense Costs   Cost incurred in the process of adjudicating a claim or suit, including defense attorney fees, the costs of expert witnesses, securing medical records, court costs, etc.

Discovery   After the reporting of an incident, claim, or suit, the discovery process focuses on the identification and collection of all facts and issues relevant to the acts or omission alleged. The process is carried out by the defense attorney assigned to the case, and this activity is protected by attorney-client privilege throughout the course of investigation, evaluation, and defense preparation.

Event/Incident Reporting   Any event involving patient injury, or an act or omission which the policyholder feels has the potential for litigation, should be reported to the insurance company immediately. The purpose of reporting is to provide early notice to the carrier, allowing creation of a claim file and assurance that coverage is in effect, and facilitating the insurer's early evaluation of the claim to control both the time and expense involved in resolving the claim.

Indemnity Payment   The amount paid to plaintiffs in resolution of a claim or suit, either in settlement or as the result of trial. Indemnity payments include actual economic losses, both past and future, and may include noneconomic damages paid to compensate an individual for physical and/or emotional pain and suffering or other abstract nonmonetary losses.

Loss Adjustment Expenses   The expense incurred by the insurance company in the investigation, evaluation, settlement, or defense of a claim or lawsuit. Most professional liability policies provide coverage for these expenses in addition to the limit of liability for indemnity payments.

Policy Endorsement   Additions to, or modifications of, the policy of insurance. Endorsements may restrict or expand coverages provided or mandated covered by the policy, address issues of corporate/partnership coverage, or modify specialty, territory, or scope of practice of the insured(s).

Policy Exclusions   Exclusions from coverage may be specified in the policy itself, or may appear as endorsements to the policy. Their effect is that the insurance company will neither indemnify nor defend actions excluded by such policy language or endorsements.

Punitive Damages   These damages may be awarded in addition to any awards for economic or noneconomic loss, and are intended to punish the defendant for flagrant or willful misconduct. While rarely awarded in medical malpractice cases, the threat of punitive damages may be used by plaintiffs in an attempt to coerce settlement of a claim.

Report Date   The date the event was reported to the insurance company, whether in the form of an incident report, report of a demand by a patient, or notice of a lawsuit. This date is important to both the insured and the company in that it triggers coverage and specifies the policy period which provides coverage.

Suit Formal filing of a claim with the court, demanding compensation from the defendant. Notice of the suit to the defendant comes with limited time for response, and must be immediately reported to the insurer to avoid incurring a default judgment (in which the court enters judgment without the defendant being able to present a defense against the allegations).

Territory The geographic area in which the policy provides coverage. It is critical that the insured inform the insurer of all locations of practice, as coverage may not apply unless that is done. In addition, premium charges may vary widely in different parts of the same state or in different states.